# "I'll Never Do That To My Kids"

## The Parenting Traps of Adult Children

by
*Carol Koffinke*

DEACONESS PRESS

Minneapolis, Minnesota

First published September, 1991

ISBN 0-925190-23-3
Library of Congress Catalog Card Number 91-072994

Cover Design by Ned Skubic, Minneapolis, Minnesota

Editor's Note: DEACONESS PRESS publishes many books and pamphlets related to the subjects of chemical dependency and mental health. These publications do not necessarily reflect the philosophy of DEACONESS PRESS, Fairview Deaconess Adolescent Chemical Dependency Programs, nor any other 12-Step Program or behavioral health program.

# CONTENTS

# DEDICATION

*TO MY PARENTS,*
*Harry and Shirley,*
*with love*

*and MY CHILDREN,*
*Julie and Richard,*
*with hope*

# ACKNOWLEDGMENTS

I wish to thank a number of people who supported me during the writing of this book. First of all, I thank my husband Dick, whose words of encouragement and vote of confidence kept me going. Next, I would like to thank my children, Julie and Richard, who never seemed to resent the time I needed to work on the computer. For opening a literary door and providing feedback on an early draft, I would like to thank my friend Dennis Daley. Also, thanks to Barbara Bluestone who never ceases to challenge me creatively.

Thanks to my parents for their love and support, and my sisters, Eva, Julie, Janet, and Chris for all we have learned from each other. Finally, I would like to thank God who brought the initial inspiration for the book to me clearly and concretely.

Chapter One

# REPLAYING THE SAME OLD TAPES

Life is not a fairytale.

Once upon a time there lived a very young princess who was kept in a tower from the day she was born. Her parents, the king and queen, visited her almost every day. During each visit, the princess begged them to let her out.

"Don't be silly, child," replied the king. "Good parents protect their children." Then they would smile and leave.

The princess was miserable, bored, and alone in her tower. She vowed that on the day she turned eighteen (when her parents no longer had any power over her), she would leave the tower and castle forever.

Finally the princess' eighteenth birthday arrived. As the tower was unlocked, the princess joyfully ran down the spiral staircase and out the front gate of the castle. As she reached the other side of the drawbridge, she abruptly stopped. All she could see was a vast countryside, void of any sign of civilization. Where would she go? How would she live? The princess quickly ran back through the gate and into the castle.

The princess had another idea. She sent messengers out to notify the neighboring kingdoms that she was in search of a husband. Before long a prince arrived, married her, and took her away to his castle.

The next year, the prince and princess joyfully gave birth to a child. The princess was determined to raise their child differently than she had been raised. But the princess was still afraid of the outside and believed that good parents protect their children. So the child was placed in a tower and the princess brought her a new toy every day.

The years slowly passed. The child wept each time she was presented with a new toy. And she begged to leave the tower. This confused the princess because she knew her child couldn't be bored with the room full of toys.

Then the princess realized that the child was probably lonely, like she had been in her own tower years ago. The next day, the princess excitedly presented the child with four puppies and three kittens. The child was elated and the princess felt good.

Soon, however, the child began to weep again and begged to be let out of the tower. The princess left in complete frustration and fell to her bed sobbing. "My poor child is miserable," she said. "What can I do?"

Suddenly, the room was filled by a bright light from which a beautiful fairy appeared. "I am your fairy godmother," the fairy explained. "I am here because you love your child and want so desperately to help her." The princess begged to be shown how she could bring happiness to her child.

"First," said the fairy, "you and your child must walk together ten feet past the front gate and remain there for a short time. Do this every day for one week. Next, you and your child are to walk together ten feet further and remain a little longer. Take a picnic, pick flowers, look at the clouds together. Do this every week, and go a little further each time. Tell your child about yourself. Listen well to what she has to say. Answer her questions honestly. Touch her. Then you and your child will be happy."

Even though she was very frightened, the princess followed her fairy godmother's instructions. Mother and child soon found this time to be the high point of their day. Feeling slightly left out, the prince asked if he could join them. They happily agreed and taught him how to be part of this special time.

The family did not live happily ever after. No one does. There were many enchanting times—but there were sad times too. The family began to understand happiness and worked to achieve it one day at a time.

§

I am not promising that this book will be your fairy godmother. However, if you are willing to look at yourself and apply what you learn, the results can be amazing. They may even seem magical.

This book will help adults examine what they were taught in their family of origin (childhood family) so that they do not perpetuate unhealthy patterns which could sabotage their efforts to create a healthy family. It will help those who are willing to make the necessary changes so their own children can grow into happy, productive adults. This book will also help adults feel secure with their parenting skills. Knowing who we are as adults and parents will increase our self-confidence.

Whether a person is or will be a parent, there most likely are some childhood issues which need examination and understanding. They *will* influence the individual's philosophy and approach to parenting. The power lies in the fact that we can "recycle"—we can take what was old and change it into something better. Successful recycling is impossible until we first identify the old patterns, become aware of the parenting traps these old patterns set up, and make the necessary changes. To avoid these parenting traps, we must examine childhood events and how we responded to them. We must also examine the impact these events had on our interpretation of life, and how they have affected our own family.

## TRUTH #1:
## Who We Are, Here And Now, Is A Product Of Where We Have Been.

You already knew this, right? It sounds so simple. But to attain what most of us want in life (happiness, love, peace, good relationships, fulfilling work), we have to take a hard look at where we have been. Who we are, who we become, and how we play out our various roles in life are products of our history. This is true regardless of which roles we examine: husband, wife, lover, friend, worker, son, daughter, and certainly parent. What have our experiences been? When did they occur? What support did we have? What values were modeled? What was our cultural background? What choices did we make? What lessons were taught? The answers are the kinds of life experiences on which we base future choices and decisions.

Our earliest teachers were our parents or guardians. So our family of origin is where we had our earliest learning experiences. And what about these teachers? What were *they* taught? What were *their* experiences? When did these experiences occur? What support did our parents have? What values were modeled? What cultural background did our parents come from? Perhaps we can get a sense of how many variables affect our development. Then —just maybe— we can begin to understand how we may find ourselves stuck in the traps from the past instead of being free to create for ourselves healthy, happy families.

Some experts believe that as many as 95% of us come from a family that was in some way dysfunctional (Friel & Friel 1989). If this is true, then most of us are probably confused as to how to raise a family that is healthy and functioning well. It is difficult for us to learn something we have not been taught. My clinical experience indicates that most, if not all, families experience problems at some time or another. A family is composed of a group of individual human beings. Not being gods, we humans have to learn as we grow. This means making mistakes, facing crises—and occasionally failing.

It is virtually impossible to have a group of individuals living together for a significant portion of a lifetime without problems arising. These problems affect all family members. That's because the family is a system of individuals linked together.

A common representation of a family system is the hanging mobile. The individual parts are interdependent. If one piece is disturbed, the other parts move as well. This is very true in a family. If one member is disturbed, other members feel some effect. If one member is removed by illness, chemical dependency, or death, the balance of the family is affected. Individuals must establish new roles and find different ways to survive and keep things going. So how long can a group of individuals live together before one is eventually disturbed by something? Not long. Yet many of us feel that if our family experiences a significant problem, someone must be doing something wrong. So let's attack this myth now.

### TRUTH #2:
### There Is No Such Thing As A Perfect Family

We pursue this goal—the perfect family—like the pot of gold at the end of the rainbow. Yet it does not exist. The quality of family life varies from day-to-day.

Let's use my own family of origin to illustrate the relative nature of this myth. For a large portion of my life my family was the one most people envied. My parents made sure my four sisters and I had nice things—even if it meant they had to go without. I had a grandmother who picked up the slack and insured that we were some of the best dressed kids in school. My parents supported us in our school activities and made sure we got good grades and learned to play the piano. One of my sisters was prom queen. My mother never worked while we were growing up and was always there when we came home from school. My father had a good job and many interests in which he involved the family. As other families experienced internal strife, my family did not. We seemed to have gone unscathed.

But by the time I was thirty years old (my youngest sister was fourteen), my family had experienced almost every crisis imaginable. One of my parents' biggest fears was that one or more of us would get pregnant before marriage. This turned out to be one of the minor challenges my family came to face. Abortion, divorce, runaways, physically abusive relationships, rape, heroin addiction, jail, and attempted suicide all visited our happy home.

Those same neighbors who had previously thought, "I wish our family could be like their family," were now sighing in relief, "Thank God our family is not like *that* family." Our family was the same group of people who once had been envied. What had changed? The situations only. Yet society perpetuates the myth that a family without problems is the healthy, normal, functional family. How are families judged? By their outward appearance—the external representation. The fact that my family survived the trauma and stuck together through it all said a lot more about us than the pretty picture we presented by getting all dressed up for church on Sundays. How crises are dealt with and resolved in our family of origin determines whether or not they are minor wrinkles or major dysfunctions.

Let's briefly look at this term "dysfunctional." This term has been used generically in the past few years and probably means something slightly different to each person. Simply defined, "functional" means to be in working order. The prefix "dys" means "bad" or "ill." So the term "dysfunctional" means "to be in poor working order." There can be many implications to this definition. Perhaps there was only one aspect of our family of origin that was not working well. Perhaps what wasn't working well happened every moment of each day. Regardless of where you plot your family, there is much to be learned from studying even one aspect that may have not been working well.

The term "Adult Child" is now used to identify an adult who grew up in some form of a dysfunctional family. It is derived from the term "Adult Child of an Alcoholic" (ACOA) which refers to an individual who was raised in a family where one or more parents were chemically dependent.

Many Adult Children realize in retrospect that something was wrong at some point in their family history—and are determined to change it in their own emerging families. They closely observe what they assume are "healthy" families to determine what is "normal."

*OK. I get it. Sunday drives in the country. Dinner together every night. No arguing. Nice clothes, home, and car. Play games together once a week. Family vacation. Good children.* These conclusions could have been drawn from observing actual people—or just as possibly, television shows.

So Adult Children try to recreate what they have observed as the signature of a healthy family. Unfortunately, what is observed is only the outward appearance, the surface behavior. This works about as well as someone trying to build an airplane from observing the outer appearance of a few they have seen. If they have never studied engines and aerodynamics, the airplane won't fly.

There is no way that an outside observer can see what happens inside a healthy family system. What happens *between* the members of that family is invisible. This invisible activity could be referred to as emotional connection. But when we observe two people holding hands we *see* what they are doing, we don't *feel* what they are feeling. Even if we sense that a family is very close to each other, how in the world are we supposed to reproduce that?

*OK, I get it. Hold hands when you walk down the street. Laugh at each other's jokes. Gaze deeply into each other's eyes.*

Television programs portraying family life have led many of us to reproduce behaviors and family activities without understanding emotional connection. If someone grew up in a family that didn't provide a healthy model to follow, then this individual will be looking for other examples of healthy family living.

How many times have you watched *The Cosby's* or *Family Ties* and wished your family could have a strong sense of togetherness and success at resolving problems? After commercials, these programs have approximately twenty minutes to create conflict and resolve it. We see much happening action-wise, but really very little emotionally. It would take much more than twenty minutes to have the emotional buildup and resolution occur in a semi-realistic way. It would be impossible in this time frame to demonstrate that some extensive communication and work was really responsible for the family getting it together—not the fact that Mom came up with some magical solution.

## TRUTH #3:
### Emotional Connection, Not Behavior, Is
### The Core Of A Healthy Family

Creating a healthy family means getting our hands dirty. We can't avoid what is happening inside the family system between the individual members. We can't avoid negative feelings or deny the reality of problems. Nor can we create healthy families without examining what's inside.

Do you have some clear ideas about what a good parent does and what good families do? Notice that I didn't say what a good parent or family *is*. When we imagine a perfect parent or family, don't we visualize a scene or some activity? Probably. Very few of us close our eyes and feel the inner workings of a happy family. We act out these scenes—or try to. That might work if we lived in a vacuum. Most of these images, however, involve others who must act out their part as well—or they will bring an abrupt halt to our fantasy. When others don't play their predetermined roles, negative feelings result.

Adult Children who come from physically abusive families provide an example of this kind of misdirected fantasy. As these individuals picture their own family, they most likely see themselves behaving much differently than their parents. It may become extremely important to see themselves as loving parents when they imagine having their own children. However, if they attempt to hold the child lovingly and the child pushes away, these Adult Children will feel a disproportionate sense of rejection. Then, because they learned to hit when feeling upset, they may strike the very child whom they were devoted to nurturing.

How much of our self-esteem is linked to successful parenting? For many adults, the very core of our happiness is dependent on how our children grow up. This could be a no-win situation if we define happiness for our children as a life free of conflict. If our children experience significant problems even in their adulthood, we automatically feel that *we* failed. When so much of our self-esteem and happiness is tied up in something we can't control, it is difficult to relax even when things are going well. Our children *will* have problems. Yet because how we validate ourselves as parents is tied to this Utopian way of life for our children, we spend a great deal of energy protecting them from conflict—even when they become adults. This prevents our children from experiencing the kind of challenges that result in personal growth and happiness.

If we could create a healthy family from the "outside in" (getting the family to reproduce the behaviors we have observed), then there would be fewer individuals identifying themselves as children from dysfunctional families. Even the active alcoholic parent, the child-abusing parent, and the sex abusing parent want to be good parents. They want to have happy children. In many cases, they can't make it happen because they don't know how. They don't realize that they have to take a hard look at themselves and change patterns from the inside out.

Taking this hard look at oneself and having a clear idea of what needs to be modified is the only way Adult Children can create a healthy family. The thread that connects family members is the emotional self.

Sharon Wegscheider-Cruse uses the hanging mobile to illustrate the family. The string and wire are the emotional sharing and awareness. The more we know ourselves—and share that real person with our family—the thicker the wire and the stronger the string. No matter what problems crop up, our family will remain together and strong.

Chapter Two

# The Solution:
# Recycling Old Responses

To change destructive patterns from the past, we first must identify them. Taking a close look at our family history will help us determine which patterns we no longer wish to perpetuate. This process will involve more work for some, and there may be some emotional pain as we look at certain aspects of growing up. But there also may be certain aspects of this history that taught positive family lessons. Either way, keep an open mind. There is the power of choice. We can keep what we choose to keep and change what we choose to change. We don't have to be victims of history just because we didn't know there was a better way.

Because there are many situations that encourage unhealthy patterns, it is impossible to cover every possible variation. However, there are distinct similarities among dysfunctional families regardless of the issues involved. The opportunity exists to apply what is presented to your particular situation.

Chronic stress can cause some degree of family dysfunction. Here is a list of common chronic stress producers:

- Chemical Dependency
- Physical Abuse

- Sexual Abuse
- Emotional Abuse
- Mental Illness
- Chronic Illness
- Death of a family member
- Change in key caretakers
- Poverty
- Workaholism or other compulsive behavior
- Chronic arguing

There are other potential traps which can create dysfunction. Here are a few examples with some important considerations:

- *Single Parenthood.* Can the parent deal with the stress of raising a child alone? How many hours a week does the parent have to work to survive financially?

- *Divorce.* How are the parents working together to address the needs of the children? How does the divorce affect the individuals financially? How does the non-custodial parent deal with this relationship?

- *Very Large Families.* Can the parents support the family emotionally and financially? At what ages are the children helping with household duties and what is the nature of their responsibilities?

- *Families with an only child.* How easily is the child able to receive whatever he or she wants? Is the child raised believing he or she is the center of the universe? Is the child encouraged toward autonomy?

Do these stress producers sound familiar? If they do, don't panic. Your history will be rich with material from which to learn. You will also have an opportunity to determine how your responses to these situations have manifested themselves in your adult life. Perhaps you find yourself on the other end of the scale with very little dysfunction. Either way, as we identify our responses to what occurred in our families, we will see why some of our efforts are not working.

The term *recycled* is appropriate here. We can focus on these dysfunctional patterns which will allow us to understand why we responded in certain ways while growing up. Then we need to determine if we are still using the same response now and if it is appropriate. If it is not appropriate, we can choose new responses once we fully understand the present - day trap that it presents. We no longer have to be a victim of the past.

Let's look at a person who grew up in a family where any expression of anger was punished. The individual has not been taught how to deal appropriately with anger, a normal healthy emotion. Once he becomes aware that this was an unhealthy family lesson, he can look at how to deal with anger in his adult life and in his role as a parent. There may be a tendency to punish the children for expressing anger, encouraging them to become compulsive people-pleasers. Perhaps he realized that this punishment was inappropriate and has attempted to change this lesson by not setting any healthy limits for his children in the expression of *their* anger. This approach may encourage them to be verbally abusive and also prevents them from learning appropriate ways to deal with anger. If the parent is willing to study his individual response to this situation as a child, and trace its impact on his adult life, he will realize that his inability to deal with anger has had negative consequences - for himself as well as his children. Then he can begin to examine new alternatives for addressing this issue.

## Mental Programming

Our brain is similar to a computer. It stores and assimilates what it is programmed to learn. As infants, our brain has only been programmed with automatic responses such as crying, sucking, and bodily functions. However, our brain is also equipped with a blank disk which records our experiences and accumulates data over time. Our brain stores this data and automatically supplies the appropriate information needed to respond to a particular situation. For example, if we, as children, tripped every time we walked through the door, we most likely will apply this experience to doors we encounter as adults. Our brain will register a door as a dangerous situation and will direct us to respond accordingly. We may avoid the door altogether, be very suspicious of it, or trip when we walk through it even if there is no one there tripping us.

This kind of mental programming is something that needs to be examined as we move toward becoming the parent we want to be. What messages were we given? What values? What rules? As in the example above, the message is *Beware of walking through doors*. If a young boy is rejected or punished every time he cries, he learns to modify this behavior. The message is *Boys don't cry*. The value is *Crying is bad*. The rule is *Don't express "soft" feelings*. The value is *Doors are bad*. The rule is *Don't trust doors*. We receive messages in our childhood which are turned into stored data in our mental computers. The circumstances surrounding these messages will be transferred into values and rules that we absorb. The result is a learned lesson in life that we will apply to future situations.

Here is a partial list of common messages that are taught in families and which are learned at a level that can affect the rest of our lives:

- Children should be seen and not heard.
- Boys don't cry.
- If you can't say anything nice, don't say anything at all.

- Nice girls don't argue (disagree, get angry).
- Girls are only good for one thing.
- Men only want one thing.
- Real men play sports (become soldiers).
- Performance is everything.
- Girls are dumber than boys.
- You are worthless (stupid, fat).
- You can't do anything right.
- You're more trouble than you're worth.
- You'll never amount to anything.
- Most things are your fault (especially Mom's or Dad's misery).
- Sex is dirty.
- You're loved only when you're good.
- Always eat everything on your plate.
- Don't tell secrets.
- Don't trust.
- Don't feel.

As you review this list, you may remember hearing some of these messages loud and clear. Mental programming is received verbally, by modeling, and by body language and facial expressions. For example, if my parents acted cold and unloving toward me every time I did something to displease them, they may not have actually *said* that they *only love me when I'm good*, but I definitely got that message. Take some time to honestly look at this list and see which messages you were programmed to receive. Perhaps you are aware of some mental programming that is not represented here. Try to take note of it with an open mind. In Chapter Four, *You the Adult*, we will explore how you have applied this mental programming to your adult life. In Chapter Five, *You the Parent*, we will look at how this affects your role as parent.

Many of these messages end up becoming legacies we leave for our children. If we were taught that sex is dirty, this will have a significant impact on our attitude toward sex, and it will influence how we mold our children's sexuality. Perhaps we will teach them the shame that we learned. Perhaps we will go to the opposite extreme and walk around the house naked all the time.

I worked with one couple who felt this was the best way to purge themselves of their sexually inhibited upbringings. It actually wasn't a problem until the husband's fourteen-year-old daughter from a previous marriage came to visit them for the summer. She felt extremely uncomfortable at the dinner table with her father and step-mother sitting in the nude. The visit was awkward and relationships strained because the adults did not modify their behavior to match the circumstance.

Let's look again at the chronic stress producers discussed earlier in this chapter. Please note that I refer to *chronic* stress. All families experience stress in some form. But coping with stress over an extended period of time usually affects family relationships. Family members change their own behavior to compensate for this stress and to maintain some balance. Picture a mobile with the string starting to unravel. Maintaining equilibrium would be very difficult. A gust of wind would likely be the end of it. Similarly we might hold our breaths and not speak about family issues lest the extreme unbalance be the death of us. This behavior is often described as walking on eggshells and is a common occurrence in dysfunctional families.

Denial is another common phenomenon in dysfunctional families. This means that something significantly wrong is happening with one or more members of the family and no one is talking about it. Denial occurs because we don't want to face reality and hope whatever is happening will disappear. However, when we deny what is happening, it becomes impossible to process the problem and find a healthy resolution. Remember, it is not the stress but our inability to deal with it that causes the dysfunction. We can't get the facts, we can't share viewpoints, we can't express feelings, we can't get support. Yet all of this is essential to the healing process. Therefore, when denial is present with a chronic stress producer, we end up pushing away the hurting part of ourselves so we can survive the situation and pain. In this way denial serves as a defense—and often a necessary one. Unfortunately, it can get recorded in our mental computer as the appropriate response to all unpleasant and painful situations we will encounter.

Our goal is to learn from the past so we can become healthy parents. You have probably identified by now the chronic stress producers in your family of origin. You should also have a fairly clear idea of what mental programming you received that may need to be changed. In the next chapter we will be looking at you—the child—as you begin this journey to become the parent you were meant to be.

Chapter Three

# You The Child

On any journey it is important to bring along certain supplies. This is equally true on our quest to become healthy parents. As you progress toward the goal of changing harmful family patterns, you will need to accumulate an awareness and understanding of who you are and how you became this person. Our purpose is not to blame but to allow ourselves the overall perspective which will assist us in making healthy decisions and healthy changes. In this chapter we will look at your life as a child and your unique responses to the chronic stress producers in your family. Gaining solid understanding of these issues will steer you toward your goal of becoming the best person and parent you can be.

## How A Dysfunctional Family Operates

Before we continue to take a look at your family from the perspective you had as a child, it is necessary to review some of the dynamics of dysfunctional families. We have learned much about dysfunctional families from studying the chemically dependent family and from the extensive work that has been done with Adult Children of Alcoholics (ACOA's). I would like to review some of this information because it is necessary to understand if we are to unravel our development as a child. (For further reading, I recommend *Another Chance*, by Sharon Wegscheider-Cruse, *Adult Children of Alcoholics*, by Janet Woititz, *It Will Never Happen To Me*, by Claudia Black, and *Co-Dependent No More*, by Melody Beattie).

When chemical dependency is evidenced in one parent, it is usually accompanied by co-dependency on the part of the other parent. Co-dependency means addiction to the alcoholic, addict, or to any person. The chemical becomes the center of the family's life. Everyone must modify himself to counterbalance the addiction. This may involve walking on eggshells or pretending to be what the addict wants so there is as little confrontation as possible. For some children it might also mean acting out to create an outlet for all the negative emotions and energy that no one is willing to focus on the addict. The addict can and usually does determine if it is going to be a good or bad day, if the other family members are happy or sad or afraid, if they can bring friends over, or even if they may sleep. Everything must be checked against this person because there is no controlling the parent's chemical use.

Family members try many creative methods to change the relationship between the addict and his chemical. Spouses mistakenly think that if they were thinner, better looking or more fun, the addict would be happier and wouldn't have to use. Children mistakenly think that if they got better grades, were more popular or were less trouble, the parent wouldn't need to use. But because this is a chronic, progressive disease, the family is not responsible for the chemical use. Families can do many things to encourage an addict to get help, but trying to change themselves to make the addict happy is not one of them. A book that addresses what does help is *Getting Them Sober*, by Toby Rice Drews.

The dynamic of co-dependency is evident to some degree in most chronic stress producers. In such cases as physical, sexual, or emotional abuse and mental illness, one parent tends to be the focal point, while the other parent spends most of his or her time and energy trying to modify family life to the situation. No one is really there for the children. Families suffering from chronic illness, death and poverty are in situations in which the stressors are not quickly changed. So the family members modify themselves, similarly to the chemically-dependent family, in order to deal with the stress.

Because one parent is cut off from the family by addiction to a chemical and the other parent is cut off by addiction to the user, the children are often left without a parent to provide consistent nurturing and positive role modeling. Children are left with the task of taking care of themselves—including the task of developing some sense of self-worth. Sharon Wegscheider-Cruse developed a model for describing the dynamics of this situation which we will briefly review.* The roles identified by Ms. Cruse and described in the following section can provide a reference to begin the process of identifying your own issues and tracing their manifestation in your adult life and your parental role.

Each description is accompanied by a set of questions to help you in this process. Try to answer them honestly. You will begin to understand how you adapted and created security/safety for yourself amidst the stress in the family.

## Family Hero

Often one child will take on the major caretaker role (usually oldest or one of the older children). Caretaking involves parenting the other children—and sometimes the parents as well. I worked with one co-dependent who admitted that her nine-year-old son was the one who reminded her to pay the bills and nagged her until she did. This is an awesome responsibility for children and tends to affect their development by rushing them into adulthood. At a time when their biggest concern should be how to find more time to play or whether or not they passed the science test, these children become trained not only to keep the household running, but also how to motivate someone else to take

*Wegscheider, Sharon. (1981). Another Chance. Science and Behavior Books, Inc. Palo Alto, CA.

care of it.  Distorted issues of control, caretaking, and hypervigilence may result.

*Hypervigilance* is a word used to describe a state of being overly aware of others and their needs at the cost of one's own self-awareness. These children learn to focus their attention on others so that they can change themselves in whatever way will best keep the peace in that situation, that particular day, with those particular people.  As these children grow up they often get into relationships where they can continue these familiar behaviors.  As they become parents, this role can become even more exaggerated.

This older child, the Family Hero, may also develop an exaggerated need to control certain aspects of his life since he is unable to control family problems.  Control provides him with a sense of security.  This need may manifest itself as overachieving in school, people-pleasing, perfectionism, or in eating disorders such as bulimia and anorexia nervosa.   It may also manifest in emotional control where most emotions are repressed.  In adulthood this learned behavior affects the quality of intimate relationships and parenting.

Consider the following questions:

1) Were you considered an overachiever as a child?
2) Were you responsible for taking care of younger children when you were growing up?
3) Did you take care of an alcoholic or addicted parent?
4) Did the rest of the family look up to and often depend upon you?

A "yes" answer to two or more of these questions indicates that your childhood response to stress was that of a Family Hero.

## Scapegoat

This role generally describes the next oldest or middle child although it could apply to any birth position. This individual often adjusts to the stress much differently than the older child. Because the Hero has taken on the responsibility of bringing respect to the family and for taking care of it, the next child is unconsciously afraid to compete with this older sibling on his turf. So he creates his own identity by behaving opposite of the Hero. There is, however, still a need for acknowledgment and control to provide some sense of security. So the Scapegoat's identity becomes tied to negative behavior which results in negative attention (but still attention that he can count on), an overall need to be different, and a thick wall of anger and defiance. This wall protects him from getting too close to anyone and from getting hurt. The Scapegoat may also be re-enacting the observed behavior of a parent and may see anger as a way to gain power and control over siblings and others much like the Hero uses overachieving and perfectionism to gain control over certain aspects of his life.

This child is often referred to as the Scapegoat because he serves as a convenient diversion for the family. Instead of facing the reality of the chemical dependency, the family can focus their negative attention elsewhere—on this child. It is safer to have a "bad kid" or troublesome brother or sister than it is to have an alcoholic spouse or parent.

Consider these questions:

1) Were you the one that got in the most trouble when you were growing up?
2) Did you receive a good deal of negative attention from parents and teachers?
3) Did you have difficulty following rules?
4) Did you tend to bully siblings and friends to get your way?

A "yes" answer to two or more of the previous questions indicates your childhood response to stress was that of a Scapegoat.

## Lost Child

There is another personality which can emerge in the family and which is usually assumed by a younger or middle child. It is often referred to as the Lost Child which is very descriptive of the way this child adjusts to the dysfunction. The Lost Child sees so much going on that he chooses solitude for safety. He can't compete with the Hero and has learned not to get in the Scapegoat's way. These children learn how to avoid conflict in a number of ways such as retreating to their room or a private place, or developing imaginary friends. They may get lost in a hobby such as reading, art, music, or models. The Lost Child provides a sense of relief for the family because he is not demanding and is fairly invisible. With only so much emotional energy to go around, this child gets left out and will not learn how to get needs met. In fact, many of these children believe that they don't really deserve to have their needs met—that they're less important than the rest of the family. How wonderful if these children could speak up and say "Hey, I need some attention." But they won't, and they will most likely receive very little nurturing.

Consider the following questions:

1) Were you considered the quiet one in the family?
2) Did you tend to leave the scene when conflict developed?
3) Did you often prefer to be alone rather than with family or friends?
4) Did you have trouble in school?

A "yes" answer to two or more of these questions indicates that your childhood response to stress was that of a Lost Child.

## Mascot

The fourth role described by Sharon Wegschieder-Cruse is the family Mascot. Frequently, the youngest child in the family will fit this role. Since this child is the youngest, he is overprotected by older siblings and parents. Older members of the family tend to protect the youngest from the emotional pain of what is happening in the family. This generally requires keeping secrets from this child. He will not get the facts as to why his brother was picked up by the police or why his father beat up his mother. In fact, when he witnesses these kinds of traumas and asks questions about them, the rest of the family will often deny what has happened. This teaches the Mascot that he cannot trust his own perception. He saw Dad hit Mom but brother said it was just his imagination. This is very confusing for this child and he grows up doubting his judgment and with a pervasive sense of fear. Put yourself in this child's place. If you couldn't make any sense out of what you know and what you see, would you perceive the world to be a very safe place? No. You would see the world as a very unpredictable place and you would not feel safe in it.

Another dynamic of the Mascot role is that these children tend to become stuck in the "cute," dependent role. The "cuteness" serves an important function for this child. It is a way of controlling the situation (lightening it up), and is a way of getting attention. Unfortunately, this Mascot role becomes compulsive for many of these individuals. They become incapable of communicating in a meaningful way, and will learn to hide their feeling behind the joke, antic, or smile. Mascots tend to remain immature and often have difficulty accepting responsibility. If they are the last child, the parents are more willing to continue to do basic things like tying shoes, buttering bread, cutting meat, and picking up after them long after they are capable of carrying out these duties themselves. Family members are less likely to expect the Mascot to contribute his share of help around the house because there are others to do it. This becomes another misdirected way of protecting the youngest from pain. *Our life is so bad that the least we can do for little Johnny is not make him do any chores.*

Consider these questions:

1) Were you considered the "clown" in the family?
2) Did you get away with situations that other children would have been disciplined for?
3) Did parents or siblings often pull your load for you?
4) Did you know you were "cute"?

A "yes" answer to two or more of these questions indicates that your childhood response to stress was that of a Mascot.

These are descriptions of the classic roles in their pure state. Could you identify with any particular role? Did you find yourself identifying with several? It is very possible that you see yourself as a blend of several roles. Maybe you actually changed roles while you were growing up. That's fine. Whatever you can learn about yourself from this model will assist you in Chapter Four when we explore adult roles, and in Chapters Five and Six when we examine parenting roles and traps.

## Other Causes of Stress

In the last chapter I mentioned how certain situations cause families to repress feelings. Repression (selectively forgetting unpleasant memories and painful feelings) is actually one of the responses to stress which causes dysfunction. This response prevents someone from processing the reality of what is happening in his life, and destroys any opportunity to deal effectively with it. It is particularly true of emotions where we must be able to express painful feelings if we are to get beyond them. Repression causes these emotions to be locked away and one can become emotionally "stuck." Let us re-examine some of the chronic stress producers in terms of emotional repression. This will provide further clues into what responses you chose as a child.

## One or Both Parents are Adult Children

If one or both of your parents were raised in a family which would fit our definition of dysfunctional, they most likely have been taught to repress feelings. Families experiencing chronic stress very seldom can deal with the powerful emotions that result. For many Adult Children, feelings of hurt, fear and emotional pain are hidden behind a myriad of defenses. That's because these feelings can cause the individual to feel vulnerable. Depending on the situation, anger can also fall into this category. If your parents learned to hide their emotional selves in order to feel safer in their family, they can only teach some form of emotional repression to you. They may not want to teach you to repress feelings and they may even change the form of what is being taught. But they *do not know* how to effectively deal with their emotional selves and therefore cannot teach it to you. The exception would be where they themselves have gotten help because their defense system has interfered sufficiently in their lives and where they hurt badly enough to try and learn a better way. An excellent book to read on this is *Grandchildren of Alcoholics*, by Ann Smith.
Consider these questions:

1) Were one or more of your grandparents an alcoholic or addict?
2) Were one of your grandparents mentally or chronically ill while your parent was growing up?

3) Have either of your parents shared the fact that he or she was physically, emotionally, or sexually abused?
4) Was either parent raised in poverty?
5) Was either parent placed in a caretaker role with siblings?

Your answers to these and all the questions in this section can help determine if you were taught to repress your feelings and which were most likely repressed.

## Presence of Emotional, Physical, or Sexual Abuse

If some form of abuse toward any member of the family existed in the home in which you were raised, it is probable that your feelings were often discounted and you were not given permission to express them. The very nature of abuse prevents expression. What would the repercussions have been if you opened up about the pain to someone who might have been able to help? Fear most likely prevented this disclosure. Many children experience shame that they somehow deserved the abuse, and fear that someone might find out how worthless they believe they really are. Both situations motivate the denial and repression of feelings. If the spouse is the victim, the feelings of hurt and anger are often denied to protect the children from the painful reality of family life. The victim often attempts to make the children "act" in certain ways which will not exacerbate the situation. If the child is the victim, they soon learn that expressing feelings associated with abuse will result in further victimization.

Abuse tends to replay itself from generation to generation as it profoundly affects the self-worth of the victim and because children learn the behavior they observe. Sometimes the child or all the children will be witnesses rather than the actual recipient of the abuse. They are still victims and they often struggle with feelings of guilt because they couldn't stop a family member's suffering, and guilt because they escaped the pain. Due to the abusive atmosphere, these feelings most likely will be unexpressed and eventually repressed. This can play out in a variety of dysfunctional ways in adult life. Extreme cases of physical, emotional, and sexual abuse can result in psychosis such as multiple personality disorder. If physical, emotional, or sexual abuse was present in your family of origin, you may find that therapy will be necessary to make the kinds of changes you want to make in your present-day life.

Consider these questions:

1) Are you aware of physical, emotional, or sexual abuse in your family of origin?
2) Do you have difficulty remembering portions of your childhood?
3) Was one of your parents excessively harsh with you but you thought you were "bad" enough to deserve it?
4) Are you aware of being afraid of one of your parents as a child?

A "yes" answer to any of these questions indicates that you may have been exposed to some form of child abuse. Look again at the feelings that are created and repressed by this chronic stress producer. These feelings provide clues as to what emotional traps await you.

### Chronic Illness

Chronic illness on the part of a family member causes feelings that are usually shamed into repression. Feeling angry, impatient or frustrated with a sick, weak, needy family member is often criticized rather that validated as a natural response. A child who expresses feelings of rejection or anger because a sick parent isn't able to care for him would most likely receive chastisement for being so selfish. Yet these are natural feelings for a child in this situation. To express fear that the person may die or never recover is usually frowned upon because it causes the family to confront the painful reality of the situation. Also, the sick individual may get the majority of attention. What child (or spouse for the matter) is going to feel comfortable expressing his own need for attention too? Not many. As a result, feelings of anger, fear, rejection and frustration as well as the expression of personal needs will be repressed.

Consider these questions:

1) Was one of your parents chronically ill?
2) Was the illness seldom discussed, particularly in terms of how it affected other family members?
3) Did you often feel that no one had time or energy for you?
4) Were you unable to express how frightened you were or how much you needed someone to look after your needs?
5) Were you a caretaker with the ill parent or younger siblings?

Affirmative answers to these questions indicate you may identify with issues and feelings associated with this chronic stress producer.

## Mental Illness

If one of your parents was diagnosed as mentally ill, he or she most likely behaved in some kind of unusual way or was a threat to himself or others. Once diagnosed, the chances are that they were hospitalized, either permanently or from time to time, and were medicated. There are forms of mental illness that can be stabilized well with medication. But a period of time had to elapse for the symptoms to manifest themselves before diagnosis was possible. A child exposed to the unusual behavior of a parent can become very frightened of that parent. The age of the child when the symptoms were active would impact the long-term consequences for the child. Trust, autonomy, self-confidence, and motivation are all issues at risk. Children often cannot share their confusion and fear because one parent is mentally ill and the other becomes addicted to that person as a caretaker. Again, there is no one from whom the child can receive emotional support and validation.

Chronic unhappiness on the part of the parent can cause a child to repress his emotional self as well. It is a monumental burden for a child to bear when a parent seldom experiences happiness. Children don't understand that the entire world does not revolve around them. They tend to be self-centered in their approach to life. If something bad happens, they tend to feel responsible in some way. This is a normal stage in their development.

However, if one of the people they look to for security and love is chronically unhappy, they will focus most of their energy on trying to make it better. This results in the typical co-dependent response where they lose touch with their own feelings and needs as they become fixated on the other person. When they begin to experience pleasure or fun, feelings of guilt arise and cannot be expressed. Feelings of inadequacy emerge when they cannot make the parent happy. Shame is felt as they conclude that they are not *good enough* to make their parent happy. To whom can they express these feelings? To the chronically depressed parent? This individual doesn't even know how to deal with his own feelings much less his child's. The other parent? This parent has most likely become co-dependent, if he wasn't already, in response to this situation which causes his or her world to center around the "sick" individual.

Consider these questions:

1) Did you have a parent diagnosed as mentally ill?
2) Did the symptoms manifest themselves while you were growing up?

31

3) Were you exposed to unpredictable behavior from this parent?
4) Did the other parent become totally focused on the ill parent?
5) Did you feel neglected in the process?
6) Would you describe one of your parents as chronically depressed or unhappy?
7) Did you find yourself frequently wondering what you did or how you could make it better?

Affirmative answers indicate that mental illness was a chronic stress producer for you as a child. Look again at the associated issues and feelings.

## Chronic Arguing

To be exposed to frequent yelling, fighting, and overall tension at home is very frightening for children. If it continues long enough, it can become "normal"—but not before the children have repressed the fear and covered up the hurt and shame. There is the fear of the loud noises and perhaps the violence associated with the fighting (breaking things, slamming doors, physical threatening). There is the fear that the parents will divorce and that the family will split up. Even if the family is dysfunctional, it is still the only family they have. They are ashamed that their family cannot get along and that there must be something wrong with them. What do they do with these feelings? Hide them just as they try to hide from the arguing. Tune out as they find ways to focus on something other than reality. Create protective walls. They know they must defend their own vulnerability if they are to survive.

Consider these questions:

1) Did your parents frequently argue/fight?
2) Was violence a part of this?

3) Were you often afraid your parents would divorce?
4) Were you afraid your parents would hurt each other?
5) Did you sometimes wish they would divorce to end all the fighting?
6) Was there no one to listen to your feelings about all of this?

Affirmative answers indicate that arguing was a chronic stress producer when you were a child. Look again at the associated issues and feelings.

## Chronic Financial Stress

When there is chronic financial stress, the atmosphere can become one of tension and worry. The children may be required to work at an early age. This situation can be fraught with jealousy because the children feel deprived, resentment because there is not enough to go around, and shame because the child cannot measure up in what unfortunately can be a very materialistic world. The expression of these emotions would most likely be interpreted as complaining, so they are not tolerated and end up being repressed. Few parents in this situation can allow the children to express their feelings. It only increases their own sense of inadequacy because they cannot provide for the family as well as they would like. Depending on how the situation is handled, the children may not react selfishly. But they may end up behaving so selflessly that they deny their own feelings and needs.

There is a great potential for loss of childhood lightheartedness (a legacy due to children) as the child gets pulled into the family plight. The ramifications can be bitterness toward life and an inability to have fun.

Consider these questions:

1) Did the lack of adequate money cause chronic stress in your family of origin?
2) Did one parent have to work more than one job?
3) Did you or any sibling have to go to work before age 16?
4) Were you embarrassed with peers because of your home or clothes?
5) Were you unable to express how it felt to be poor?
6) Did you often give up things you wanted so that others in the family could have what they wanted?

Affirmative answers indicate that financial difficulties were a chronic stress producer when you were a child. Look again at the associated issues and feelings.

## Death Of A Family Member

Even though the death of a family member is not a chronic situation, dealing with the resulting emotional pain can take so long that it becomes a chronic stress producer in the family. Whether the loss involves a parent, spouse, or child, the pain is so acute that some people tend to hide and repress their own feelings. They may fear the painful feelings, or they may attempt to spare others additional pain. How many people have you heard say, "I had to be the strong one." The surviving parent holds back his grief in front of the children in an attempt to protect them. This, however, may discount the fact that grief is a natural response.

If the death involves a child, many surviving siblings struggle with the guilt that they were not the one who died. They think, *Mom and Dad must have loved Johnny so much. Maybe it would have been better if I had died instead.* Parents may be unavailable emotionally for their children as their own emotions are overwhelming. Sometimes the only option for the parent or surviving children is some degree of emotional shutdown.

The loss of a loved one may also result in feelings of anger on the part of the survivors that the individual abandoned them. This anger is difficult to express because it seems so selfish. Whether or not the child is given permission to express all the feelings and whether or not an individual is available emotionally for him will determine the extent of repression.

Consider these questions:

1) While you were growing up did the death of a parent, brother, or sister occur?
2) Were you able to express your anger, fear, hurt, and guilt to someone?
3) Did you feel a part of the family during this time, or excluded/alone?
4) Did you attend the funeral?
5) Did you cry?
6) Do you feel your family dealt with the loss and was eventually able to function as a family again?

Use these questions to determine if you and your family grieved and then moved on. If you answer "no" to most of these questions, the issues and feelings may have set traps for you in adulthood.

### Compulsive Behavior on the Part of the Parent

A parent exhibiting compulsive behavior is similar to a chemically dependent parent. But instead of using chemicals, compulsive parents focus on something outside of themselves to distract their internal problems and medicate emotional pain. The non-addictive spouse becomes caught in the web of the compulsion as energy is consumed in caretaking and enabling behaviors. Feelings of hurt, anger, fear, and frustration are repressed as they attempt to connect with one who is emotionally anesthetized. Where are the children? They're left with two parents whose ability to connect with them on an emotional level are limited, and who are unlikely to help them validate their own emotional selves.

Consider these questions:

1) Would you describe either of your parents as a compulsive gambler, workaholic, or TV addict?
2) Was this parent unavailable to you or the family as a result?
3) Did your other parent become unavailable to you because most of their energy was tied up with either fixing the compulsion or covering up and protecting the compulsive parent?

If you answer "yes" to these questions, you should be able to relate to the issues and feelings associated with the chemically dependent family.

## Now What?

The survival skills you developed as a child don't just disappear when you reach age eighteen. The first step is becoming aware of your response in your family of origin. That is what you have learned. Unless you have had other teachers since then, you probably have not learned another way to deal with problems, stress, yourself, and life.

Consider these questions:

1) What feelings did you repress as a child?
2) How did you deal with the situation emotionally?
3) What behavior emerged?
4) Where did you seek to establish control in your life?

Exploring these questions will help you gain an understanding of what traps may lie ahead. The feelings identified will be the ones you have the most difficulty expressing. How you dealt with each situation will indicate what defense systems you developed. How you established control to create a feeling of safety will indicate possible control issues to be dealt with in adulthood.

We will now continue on our journey and examine ourselves as adults. This is an important step before we attempt to understand our parenting traps. Refer to what you have learned about yourself so far. It will be helpful throughout the next several chapters.

Chapter Four

# You The Adult

As we seek clues to discover who we are, it is often easier to recognize behavioral patterns because they are visible and tangible. We are made up of behaviors (physical action), thoughts (mental action), feelings (emotional action), and soul (spiritual action). Of these kinds of action, behavior (physical action) is the most observable.

Because behavior is visible, it becomes helpful to identify ourselves as a kind of behavioral stereotype. This will give us clues as to what may lie beneath. Most of us are less aware of our emotional selves than our behavioral selves although we may be reluctant to examine either part honestly. For example: If I asked you to describe your self emotionally, where would you begin? I could ask if you feel angry or depressed frequently but some feelings become defenses behind which others hide. Suppose, however, I asked you if you worry a lot, joke a lot, try to be the best at everything you do, or work to have everyone like you. You could answer "yes" or "no" with a little more conviction. These behaviors help identify needs which can lead you to your feelings. This is what we need to explore.

It is important to understand our emotional selves if we are to change dysfunctional patterns in our lives. Try to keep an open mind for the moment as I ask you to stereotype your behaviors (not you, just your behaviors). Remember you are more than what you *do*. You may find that you identify with several of the behaviors described below. That's fine. There is something to be learned from each.

## Classic Roles in Adulthood

Let's take a look at how the four classic roles (Family Hero, Scapegoat, Lost Child, Mascot) have manifested themselves in adulthood. We will examine how the childhood issues play themselves out in adulthood. You have most likely identified your child of the past with one or more of these roles. Read the following descriptions of their adult manifestations and see if you can relate to one or several. This understanding will give you some insight into your adult recovery issues. In the next chapters we will examine their impact on your role as a parent. I have separated some behaviors which may be similar because each brings a separate set of issues to the parent-child relationship. It will be beneficial to understand each of the behavior types separately so that they can be examined again later. It is probable that you will identify with more than one of these adult behaviors.

### Overachiever/People-Pleaser

This behavior is very similar to the Family Hero described in the last chapter. Overachiever/People-Pleasers take life very seriously and overextend themselves, always trying to be the best at everything. They will overachieve at work, at home, with family and with friends and often end up feeling burnt out. These people have a strong need to be liked by others. They try to create an identity through outside positive reinforcement such as promotions, raises, and pats on the back. Sometimes these individuals will become physically ill as they push themselves beyond the realm of human potential.

Emotionally, these individuals struggle with tremendous guilt. They feel guilty if they make a mistake, or say something that someone doesn't like. They set themselves up for an ongoing unconscious source of guilt. No one can meet the standards they set for themselves. No one is perfect and no one can make everyone like him or her. This contributes to a continuous sense of inadequacy—compensated by further attempts at overachieving. These individuals seldom express anger. It is viewed as an undesirable emotion and they are unwilling to do anything that could remotely be interpreted as undesirable. Their inability to deal with emotions, especially negative ones, will prevent them from engaging in truly intimate relationships.

Consider these questions:

1) Do you as an adult have difficulty disagreeing with others?
2) Do you have difficulty expressing anger?
3) Do you tend to overachieve in the majority of endeavors?
4) Are you hard on yourself for not doing better, even when others have told you that you have done well?
5) Do you often feel guilty when not doing well enough?
6) Do you work hard to keep partner relationships intact?

Affirmative answers indicate that you identify with the Over-achiever/People-Pleaser and the associated issues.

## Perfectionist

The behaviors described in the section above may very well be coupled with perfectionism but not all perfectionists are people pleasers. Therefore, this behavior will be explored separately although there are many similarities.

The Perfectionist is an overachiever. But their high standards are projected onto others which tend to negatively impact their relationships. Perfectionists are usually hypercritical of the world. Very few people do things the best way they can be done. The situation may involve stirring a pot with the proper spoon, preparing a report which is thorough enough, or governing the country with the proper philosophy.

Emotionally, the Perfectionist often feels frustrated and impatient with others. They will use this behavior to distract themselves from feelings such as hurt and fear which lead to a frightening sense of vulnerability. Like the "Controller" (see below) these individuals often maintain an authoritative or parental role in partner relationships. Please note that I don't use the word "intimate." These people unconsciously use perfectionism to protect themselves from getting too close to others. As they put others down and see themselves as better, a considerable gap is formed and there is no chance for intimacy. These individuals attempt to fill their inner selves by continually trying to create a perfect outer world. This compensates and distracts them from a chaotic and imperfect inner world.

Consider these questions:

1) Do you find yourself consistently setting high standards for yourself and others?
2) Would you consider yourself a critical person?
3) Do you feel somewhat out of control when others don't follow your guidance?
4) In partner relationships, do you tend to act like the parent in that you try to teach and guide your mate to the best he or she can be?
5) Do you have difficulty allowing yourself or others to relax and perhaps make mistakes?

Affirmative answers indicate that you identify with the Perfectionist and the associated issues.

## Controller

These individuals need to have life unfold according to their plan. Their behavior is often outwardly bossy but can also hide behind subtle manipulation. Controllers experience a strong need to have things done *their* way and respond with anger, resentment, hurt, and feelings of rejection when others don't cooperate. This comes from an unconscious fear of being out of control, and manifests as a compulsive need to control what's happening around them (how people dress, talk, wear their hair, behave, perform, make decisions, think, and feel). Messages given out to family members are, "If you really loved me, you'd do it my way" and, "When you do things my way, it's a sign that you love me." These people try to fill their inner selves by creating a sense of security and power by having the world unfold according to their design. This kind of behavior can easily, but not always, be coupled with the Perfectionist.

In partner relationships, these individuals will usually maintain an authoritative, dominant role. They are attracted to those who cooperate either willingly or unwillingly with their need to have things their way. The approach, however, may be more subtle and manipulative in which case they may appear to take a back seat. The relationship between controller and follower has a gap which prohibits true intimacy.

Consider these questions:

1) Do you find yourself spending a lot of energy getting others to do things your way?
2) Do you feel a sense of rejection when others don't cooperate with you?
3) Do you have difficulty giving up when someone wants to do something differently than you think he should?
4) Do you feel uncomfortable around independent people?

5) Does your history of relationships include partners who you could dominate or who had difficulty standing up for their rights?

Affirmative answers indicate that you identify with the Controller and the associated issues.

## Caretaker

These people have a strong need to take care of others to the point where an enormous amount of responsibility for family members, friends, and neighbors is assumed. Caretakers tend to parent their mate but differently than the Perfectionist. They don't try to get their partners to do it their way—they just do it for them. Caretakers will often do for others that which they are quite capable of doing for themselves. These individuals try to fill their inner self by having others need them and by making life easier for others. To a certain extent, this can be a beautiful quality in an individual (as many of these roles can be). But often this quality is taken to the extreme where one's own needs are neglected and where others are encouraged to remain dependent.

Caretakers often struggle with feelings of guilt for not doing enough to insure the happiness and success of others. They may become resentful when people don't appreciate their efforts. Feelings of being overwhelmed and inadequate are common. Caretakers often marry alcoholics, addicts, or some form of Baby (see upcoming section). Physically or emotionally ill partners are also attractive to the Caretaker. This kind of a relationship provides a natural outlet for their need to be responsible for others. At some point the martyr role may become very comfortable for these individuals. They eventually are victimized by their need to care for others and believe they are incapable of significantly modifying this need.

Consider these questions:

1) Are you attracted to needy individuals?
2) Do you "parent" your partner, treating him or her as a dependent child?
3) Do you feel responsible for the success and happiness of others?
4) Do you find yourself seeking ways to become involved in others' lives?
5) Do you feel guilty taking time out for yourself?

Affirmative answers indicate that you identify with the Caretaker and the associated issues.

### Rebel

Like the Scapegoat, these individuals learn that the best way to feel safe is to keep people at a distance, and to be different enough to insure that they don't get lost in the crowd. These individuals will be rebellious and defiant, even in adulthood, and are easily angered. Rebels are resistant to being part of the norm either by their appearance, behavior, or both.

Emotionally, these individuals cover up most feelings by expressing anger, regardless of the emotion being experienced. This is particularly true with the softer feelings of hurt and fear which cause the Rebel to feel vulnerable. Covering these emotions with anger serves the same purpose in adulthood as it did in childhood. It prevents people from getting too close by encouraging them to keep their distance. This "distancing" behavior distracts the Rebel from his own sense of vulnerability by projecting an image of invincibility.

The Rebel attempts to fill his inner self by creating a sense of power that unfortunately results in keeping others away and turning people

Carol Koffinke

off.  Authority figures may pose a threat in adulthood just as they did
in childhood, resulting in work or legal problems.   In partner
relationships, these individuals insist on being dominant.  They are
attracted to those who are incapable of asserting themselves and
expressing their needs.  They may continue to bully others and may
even use violence to insure their control.

Consider these questions:

1) Is anger the feeling you express the most?
2) Do you respond to direction from supervisors with anger
   and resentment?
3) Do you secretly resent doing things other people's way?
4) Do you pick arguments and fights with others?
5) Do you feel panicky when others try to usurp your authority?
6) Does this sometimes lead to violence or screaming to keep
   your position?
7) Do you find yourself trying to be "different" by seeking
   negative attention?
8) Do you intimidate your partner to maintain a certain
   dominant status?

Affirmative answers indicate that you identify with the Rebel and
associated issues.

### Doormat

I use this term not in a judgmental way but because many of these
individuals with whom I have worked refer to themselves as "Doormats."  Although the term has more of a negative connotation than
some of the others, I  use it only because it assists the behavior
identification process.

46

The feelings of being unimportant carry over into adulthood for the untreated Lost Child. These individuals feel confused about their rights and needs and they struggle to assert themselves. They flounder regarding their life's work, have difficulty making decisions, have difficulty establishing goals, and do not fit in well anywhere. There is a part of the Doormat that remains the Lost Child—needy yet unable to ask, lonely but unable to connect.

The Doormat may have Loner traits. Feelings of loneliness, inadequacy and fear motivate them to avoid situations where they will most likely fail at meaningfully connecting with others. Safety is in loneliness. When Doormats marry, they will compromise themselves at all costs to maintain calmness and to avoid any conflicts. Partners tend to be those who seek a position of dominance and who avoid intimacy. These individuals attempt to fill their inner self by avoiding situations where the inadequacy is felt. Safety is in compliance.

Consider these questions:

1) Do you have difficulty asserting and expressing your needs?
2) Do you prefer to be alone?
3) Do you feel insecure when others try to get close?
4) Do you often feel uncomfortable in a crowd?
5) Do you envy other people's self-confidence?
6) Do you frequently avoid social situations?
7) In partner relationships, will you do anything to
   keep the peace?

Affirmative answers indicate that you identify with the Doormat and the associated issues.

Carol Koffinke

## Entertainer

You know this person as the office clown or perhaps the life of the party. Energy is spent in entertaining others and keeping situations happy and light. These individuals work hard for outside validation in the form of laughs and attention. The Entertainer is an untreated Mascot. Joking around and playfulness will continue to serve as a defense and a way to avoid intimacy with others. Entertainers easily attract others because they are outgoing and "cute." Partners will admire their sense of humor and social ease and will overlook the fact that they may be lackadaisical about bills, work and neatness. Entertainers attempt to fill their inner-self by being popular.

Consider these questions:

1) Are you usually considered the "life of the party"?
2) Do you have difficulty maintaining a serious conversation?
3) Do you feel a need to lighten up situations which are serious or quiet?
4) Do you use your social ease and winning personality to get your way with others?
5) Do you feel uncomfortable when partners want to talk about problems or serious issues?

Affirmative answers indicate that you identify with the Entertainer and the associated issues.

## Baby

As an adult, these individuals lag behind their peers in responsibility and independence. They will have difficulty assuming the adult role and will depend on friends and partners. Babies have difficulty keeping jobs or establishing careers. Emotionally, these individuals may appear to be weak and helpless. In reality, they are usually adept at creating situations where their needs are met by others. Babies may have Entertainer or Loner characteristics. In either case, they will most likely seek partners who are caretakers to compensate for their own lack of independence and responsibility. Remaining the eternal child creates a sense of safety for these individuals. This is how they fill their inner-self. Being cared for by others makes them feel safe.

Consider these questions:

1) Do you dislike having responsibilities and frequently leave them unattended?
2) Do you depend on others to "pick up the slack"?
3) Do you link up with those who are willing to take care of you?

Affirmative answers indicate that you identify with the Baby and the associated issues.

### Worrier

Several of the other behaviors can be combined with this one. These individuals are in a chronic state of worry. If there is nothing immediate to worry about (marriage, children, health, friends, or money), they will project their fear into the future, worrying about what their life—and other's—will be like in ten or twenty years. Their approach to life is strongly based in fear. A Worrier may be an untreated Mascot, Lost Child or even Family Hero.

Worriers attempt to fill their inner selves by compulsively obsessing on negative possibilities. This allows them to focus outside of themselves—which is unconsciously perceived as a very scary place. Feelings of fear are familiar to the Worrier and therefore safer than maintaining peace of mind. Anxiety is experienced when these people are faced with a lack of distracting issues. Worriers tend to partner with individuals who will assist them in their need to worry. Stable, healthy relationships are unconsciously avoided.

Consider these questions:

1) Are you often in a state of worry?
2) Do you feel uncomfortable when everything is going well?
3) Do you seek out relationships which are ripe for problems?

Affirmative answers indicate that you identify with the Worrier and the associated issues.

## Taking a Look at Our Journey

Let's put together everything we have covered. You most likely identified with one or more of the four classic roles reviewed in Chapter Three. Having read the possible manifestations of these roles in your adulthood, perhaps you are beginning to understand how your childhood issues play out in the present.

Consider these questions:

1) Were you a Family Hero who became an Overachiever?
2) Were you a Family Hero who became a Perfectionist?
3) Were you a Family Hero who became a Caretaker?
4) Were you a Scapegoat who became a Rebel?
5) Were you a Scapegoat who became a Controller?
6) Were you a Scapegoat who became a Perfectionist?
7) Were you a Lost Child who became a Loner?
8) Were you a Lost Child who became a Worrier?
9) Were you a Lost Child who became a Baby?
10) Were you a Mascot who became an Entertainer?
11) Were you a Mascot who became a Baby?
12) Were you a Mascot who became a Worrier?

Although there are other possible combinations, these are the most likely. However, it is possible that circumstances in your adult life have resulted in a total switch of roles. So don't limit your perception by the above questions. Be as honest as you can with yourself.

Several other elements of our lives need to be examined before we can become well-prepared for the next leg of our journey. These elements can become serious issues for us in adulthood.

## Enmeshment

Enmeshment is fairly common in dysfunctional families. The term means that there is a lack of boundaries between two individuals. Instead of two people bringing their own identities into a relationship, the two blend and respond to life as one. This may sound like an ideal connection to some, but as we will see, enmeshment has a negative impact on relationships.

Enmeshed relationships often evolve in dysfunctional families due to an environment that stifles identity formation. In healthy families, the energy is expended in addressing the individual needs of the family members. Chronic stress producers can force family members to use their energy to modify themselves in order to survive the stress. *What do I need to do to avoid the fear?* This pursuit does not usually leave much for self-exploration. Due to the lack of identities, parents and children often become enmeshed in these situations. Enmeshment is also a common dynamic between addict and co-dependent.

If there are no identities, it is difficult to establish individual boundaries. Becoming enmeshed with another individual or individuals can be a way of trying to complete ourselves because we feel so empty. It can be a way of trying to find ourselves because we feel so lost. We think merging with another is the answer to fulfillment, love and happiness.

When we grow up unable to form a sense of our own identity, we often seek relationships in adulthood where we can become enmeshed in someone else's identity. The result, however, is that we become a victim to someone else's life—a life over which we have no control. The fact that we may concentrate all our energy on the relationship doesn't matter. The reality is that it still is someone else's life. We can't shape another's life to satisfy our need to feel safe. A relationship does not consist of an individual or even two individuals. What happens *between* the two individuals constitutes the relationship. The very nature of the word *relationship* indicates that something must occur between at least two entities. Each individual brings themselves to the other. The sharing of self results in intimacy. In enmeshed relationships one is merely the shadow of the other.

In an enmeshed relationship, my happiness is dependent on yours. Your life is my life. Your needs are my needs. This takes away all personal power because we are tied to someone whom we can never fully control. I cannot make you successful, happy, or loving. If you don't take it upon yourself to do these things, I become a victim to your inability to do so. It is much healthier for me to take responsibility for my own needs and happiness and bring my self to you in our relationship. I create personal power for myself and I relieve you of a mighty burden. Enmeshment can occur in partner relationships, parent-child relationships, friendships, and even in working relationships.

As they approach adulthood, many children may attempt to physically or verbally cut themselves off from their families due to anger toward the parents. The emotional ties to the parents, however, are often very powerful even after the child moves away or ceases communication. Adult Children may still evaluate their lives through their parents' perceptions due to this process of enmeshment and the absence of their own identity. They may find themselves consciously or unconsciously considering what Mom or Dad would think of what they are doing. There will be some form of guilt if it's different from what they were taught to believe as acceptable. This situation is often observed in the chemically-dependent family where the recovering Adult Child experiences considerable guilt as he moves into recovery while the parents remain locked in their chemical dependency or co-dependency. Feelings of loss are also experienced because he can no longer belong to the "family." Dysfunctional family ties are often more like shackles than those in healthy families because of the enmeshment. It is sometimes difficult to understand why an abused child grows up defending his abusive system. There is an unconscious fear. *If they're bad, then maybe I am too.*

Enmeshment may even be present in situations where an Adult Child rebels against his parents. *If Mom wants me to marry that kind of man, I'll show her.* Or, *If Dad wants me to follow the family tradition and become a doctor, I'll show him.* Even though he or she may have decided to go against family norms, the focus is still on the parents. Decisions are still being calibrated against what Mom or Dad wants or doesn't want. We will talk more about this when we examine our parenting.

Consider these questions:

1) As an adult do you still seek verbal approval from a parent on issues as simple, for example, as what sofa you select?
2) Do you look to a parent or partner to make most of your decisions?
3) Do you find yourself doing the opposite of what a parent would have you do?
4) Do your parents still have the ability to ruin your day?
5) Do you find that your moods are dependent on the moods of a partner or parent?
6) Do you refrain from participating in an activity that your partner is not involved in, particularly if he or she is critical of it?

Affirmative answers to the previous questions indicate a tendency toward enmeshment. This dynamic may play out in many of your relationships—including the relationship with your children—unless you come to terms with it.

## Injured Child

Children need physical, emotional, and mental nurturing during the developmental years to properly grow physically, emotionally, and mentally. It has been well documented that baby animals who are deprived of physical contact with either another animal or human, but who are still fed and have all other needs met, will die. Children also need an overall sense of safety and security. This allows them to stretch their limits as they take risks in a multitude of areas without fear of rejection, loneliness, even death. If children do not feel reasonably safe and are not nurtured, they become injured inside.

The Injured Child cannot continue to grow into a secure, responsible adult even if he has matured physically. This adult has a child locked inside. The inner child warps this individual's perception and interpretation of the world. The needs that the child would have normally had gratified during the developmental process (affection, encouragement of initiative, positive reinforcement, and a sense of security) are still unmet and beg for gratification. These needs must be fulfilled if the child is to develop a healthy sense of autonomy. As the body grows but the child's needs are ungratified, that child becomes developmentally stuck. Thus we see a 35-year-old woman interpreting life through the eyes and emotions of a five-year-old, or perhaps a 60-year-old man still looking for the validation and security of a small child.

Children, however, can ask openly to have their needs met. They have not yet had to build an intricate defense system to survive. Children will ask, "Do you love me, Mom?" "Will you play with me,

Dad?" "Will you hug me?" The fear of rejection has not yet hampered their direct approach to need gratification. Some adults with the Injured Child inside will still try the direct approach. But they will interpret all negative responses as personal rejection instead of being able to understand that the other person may be tired or has had a bad day. Others develop an intricate system of games in an attempt to meet the same needs. *Have I done well enough to become worthwhile? Have I made enough people dependent upon, me for me to be needed? Do enough people think I'm the greatest so I know I'm lovable? Am I desired enough sexually to know I'm OK?* The answer to all of these questions is no—a hard, emphatic, chilling no. It's *never* enough. When our Injured Child pushes us to seek outside validation for our lovability or worth, we find ourselves on a never-ending quest. That's because our inner lack of self-worth will negate all the outside positive validation. We can only get that kind of validation from one place—ourselves. We have to be the ones who know we are worthwhile, lovable, trustworthy individuals capable of providing for all our needs.

How do we validate ourselves? We must find out who we really are. We must stop running away from the *fear* of finding out who we really are. And we must stop running away from the pain. It can be difficult for many of us to look really hard at our Injured Child because we will be forced to encounter all the pain from the past. For many of us, this will mean therapy. We have to go back and allow the Injured Child to do the necessary work to heal the wounds. Then, when the wounds are healed, the Injured Child can grow. With help, the pace of growth will occur much faster then it would naturally. We have the intellectual ability, motivation, and attention span to capitalize on our adulthood and grow, grow, grow inside. Isn't it worth the risk?

I have learned something very powerful from the hundreds of groups I have run ... when we take the risk to explore who we are and share that with another human being, we begin to experience our beauty and divinity. This is an important step in the process of learning self-love. How can we love someone we don't know? How can we trust someone we don't know? The self-awareness process enables us to feel safe within ourselves. Once we feel safe within ourselves, we can begin to feel safe in the world.

If you are an untreated Adult Child, there is a good possibility that somewhere inside of you is an Injured Child.

Consider these questions:

1) Do you sometimes wonder why you react in extremes to certain situations?
2) Are you aware of a strong need for outside validation?
3) Do you often feel out of control of your emotions and/or behavior?

Affirmative answers indicate the presence of an Injured Child. If one is present, the Injured Child must be allowed to heal and grow. Failure to do so will have a negative impact on your attempts to become a healthy parent.

## Control Issues

In Chapter Three, we examined the four classic roles and how each child found a way to establish some sense of control in his life to create a feeling of safety: the Family Hero by overachieving and caretaking, the Scapegoat by being different and distancing others, the Lost Child by isolating, and the Mascot by laughing everything off. Most children from dysfunctional families have applied the need to establish control to their emotional selves as well. They will learn to repress a variety of feelings depending on the conditions in their family of origin. This serves the dual purpose of providing protection from emotional pain and creating an area where they can count on full control. A typical case is one where a young boy will refuse to cry regardless of the physical or verbal abuse he receives. The adult may manifest this repression by not even allowing himself to cry over the death of a parent or child. While the individual has temporarily protected himself from emotional pain, the unresolved grief will cause other problems as it continually raises its head in an attempt to be expressed.

The need for control remains strong in adulthood for several reasons. One is that the Injured Child did not have the need for a safe environment fulfilled during the developmental years. As we have seen, the Injured Child still has a need to create safety for himself even in the adult body. This need will cry out for constant gratification. Establishing control over one's external world is one attempt to gratify this need. Also, it most likely became a factor in pure survival in the family of origin. This, of course, is not suddenly unlearned when someone reaches age eighteen.

In adulthood, this need for control will often find itself manifesting itself in relationships. Any and all relationships are subject to this issue: partner, parent-child, co-worker, friend. The behavior may appear in the form of one who always has to have his or her own way. It may, however, evidence itself in subtle manipulations, where the Adult Child is not demanding but uses guilt, or some other passive method to manipulate others to follow suit.

Consider these questions:

1) Do you respond to a variety of situations with the same emotion?
2) Do you often cry when anger would seem to be the more appropriate response? (control anger)
3) Do you often get angry when you have been hurt or are afraid? (control feelings of vulnerability)
4) Have you identified yourself as a Controller, Rebel, or Perfectionist?

Use this section and these questions to help determine where you need control. Identify what you need to maintain control over in order to feel safe. The parent/child relationship is fraught with challenges to your control. Unless you become aware of your control issues, a trap is created which sets up a repressive situation for your child—and a no-win situation for you.

## Moving On

In this chapter you explored your adult role as it emerged from your family origin and childhood responses. You probably were able to see some patterns and similarities in yourself as a child and your adult role. Perhaps you are beginning to understand some adult issues that need addressing.

Consider these questions:

1) What adult roles are you playing now?
2) Are you in an enmeshed relationship with a parent or partner?
3) What control issues have you identified?

Answer these questions as best you can before going on the next leg of our journey. The answers will identify what traps may await you in parenthood. We will work together to avoid them.

Chapter Five

# PARENTING TRAPS

Thus far our journey has brought us to the point where we can utilize personal insights and apply them to our role as parent. This is another key step in our quest to change certain family legacies. We have explored the chronic stress producers that existed in our family, and how we responded to them as children in order to create a sense of safety. We also examined what was modeled and taught to us by our earliest teachers—our parents. Next we explored how these lessons were carried into adulthood and affected our interpretation and approach to the world.

There are six general parenting traps that ensnare many Adult Children: overcompensation, inability to set healthy boundaries, overprotection, vicarious living (a form of enmeshment), perfectionism, and rigidity. You will explore these issues on a personal level so that your own entanglement becomes apparent.

## Overcompensating

Many of us are aware of what we did not like about our childhood, at least on a superficial level. As we discussed in Chapter One, it is difficult to evaluate the inner workings of a healthy family. This is complicated by the fact that most of us are assessing the family structure from the Injured Child's point of view.

So how do Adult Children respond? We get out our magnifying lens, decide what was wrong, then we vow we won't make the same blunders as we create our own families. Here are some examples:

- My family was too strict.
- My family was too lenient.
- We were spoiled rotten.
- We were deprived (emotionally, physically, financially).
- There was too much arguing.
- We were not allowed to express our feelings.
- My parents never attended my games or activities.
- My parents were never home.
- There was no privacy.

It has been well established by Janet Woititz and other recovery professionals that Adult Children feel safest working with concrete concepts that are either black or white, right or wrong, good or bad. As we develop our own parenting philosophy, we take whatever we have attached ourselves to as *the* culprit in our "jaded" childhoods—then flip it 180 degrees. The rationale is this: if left is wrong (bad), then right must be correct (good). That thinking would make sense if we are traveling toward a town and we hit a fork in the road. One way will get us there and the other won't.

As Adult Children, however, we extend this thinking into a new, workable parenting philosophy. If strict is evaluated as wrong then the more strict the parent, the worse that parent is. Conversely, lenient would be right. The more lenient the parent, the better.

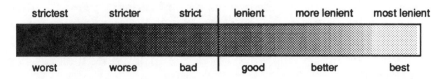

This conclusion may not be a fully conscious one. We may say that one should not be *too* permissive. Yet when we start to set a limit with our children, our old programming kicks in. As we say "no" we become consciously aware of sounding like Mom or Dad and pull back. Because we think in black and white terms, we are unable to comfortably set the limit lest we prostitute our ethical standards. These standards have been formed as a reaction to what we have determined healthy versus dysfunctional in our family.

Here is a similar situation:

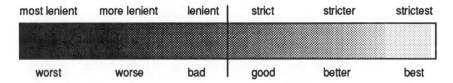

The same principle applies to whatever we concluded was "wrong" in our family. What some Adult Children assess as the negative influence in their family may be the opposite of what others assess.

Several years ago I led a group for co-dependents, some of whom were parents who had a chemically dependent child in treatment. One set of parents, John and Mary, insisted that they were so strict, overprotective, and smothering, their son rebelled by becoming an addict. Another set of parents, Tom and Ann, insisted they had been too permissive in not setting enough limits for their son. He ended up getting involved with the wrong crowd and eventually got hooked on drugs. Upon looking into the parents' family histories, I found that they were each brought up contrary to the way they were parenting their children. John and Mary each described their families of origin as totally lacking supervision while Tom and Ann described their families as oppressive.

Each set of parents concluded that their methods had been unsuccessful on the sons in treatment, even though the approaches were very different. Had these individuals not been involved in a group, they most likely would have overcompensated again by swinging 180 degrees. They had already overcompensated once, in reaction to their families of origin. To do the right thing, they thought they had to take giant steps in the opposite direction. This kind of thinking can result in a situation frequently observed in dysfunctional families: total chaos or dictatorship. Balancing the two extremes seems too complicated, confusing, and scary for many Adult Children.

Consider these questions:

1) What about you? Can you identify some ways that you overcompensate?
2) What would you change about the way you were raised?
3) How do you deal with these issues differently with your own children?

Plot the issues using the following graph format:

| Trait I would change. | | | | | Response with my children. | | | |
|---|---|---|---|---|---|---|---|---|
| 5 | 4 | 3 | 2 | 1 | 2 | 3 | 4 | 5 |

(Plot how extreme the trait was)    (Plot how extreme you are)

Example: You were brought up in a home where you could not express anger.

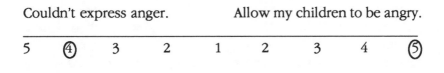

Couldn't express anger.  Allow my children to be angry.

Perhaps you selected a "4" for the left side of the graph because you were not able to show anger, disagree, or challenge your parents in any way. A "5" may not have been selected, perhaps, because there was no physical abuse involved in the molding of this behavior. On the right hand side of the graph, you may have plotted a "5" because you allow and encourage your children full expression of anger without any guidance to teach them what is and is not appropriate behavior. Fear of teaching them to repress their anger may have been the motivation behind this restraint on your part.

A graph that really indicates the happy medium and the healthy boundaries of the behavior looks like this:

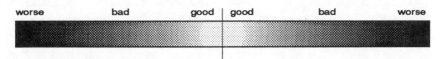

This graph illustrates the "gray" area as opposed to our old graph which illustrates the "black and white" thinking.

We need to find the happy medium. There have to be limits. Our children can be too spoiled (an overcompensation if we were deprived), or too deprived (an overcompensation if we were spoiled). They can be rude and inappropriate when expressing themselves or too afraid to open their mouths. We can drive ourselves crazy trying to attend every game/show/activity, participating in every meeting, chaperoning every dance, and baking for every bake sale and party because our parents never were involved. We can force ourselves to stay home with the children until they are eighteen years old because *our* parents both worked and weren't there for us. (This would be a healthy decision if the decision was based on our own needs and desires, not as an overcompensation for what we perceived our parents did wrong.) We can be so afraid of prying into our children's affairs that we avoid asking the necessary questions to get a sense of what is happening in their lives.

Any trait, when taken to extreme, loses its virtue. Take generosity, for example. It is a wonderful trait. But if you give away *everything* you and your family possess, you have taken the trait to the point where it hurts yourself and others.

When we know who we are, we will trust our judgement. We will become aware of our own needs and desires as well as those of our children. We will no longer react to the past but deal effectively with the present. We will feel safe enough to assess our children's needs individually, to blend our experience, fears, and hopes into an approach that will work for us as well as our children.

My parents grew up with little family structure. In fact, my father had none. He came and went as he pleased, even as a young child. As young parents, my mother and father were determined to do things differently. I was the first-born, so they were able to practice their new parenting philosophy on me. My bedtime was 6:00 PM until the age of seven, and even at age eleven I remember being in bed in the summer while it was still light outside. I was spanked for being late for dinner and would have to sit at the table as long as it took to finish my meal. My parents were not trying to torture me or make me miserable. They just wanted to be *sure* that I had enough sleep and ate well so that I would be healthy. As a reaction to the lack of structure in their families, life became rigid around issues of schedules and rules.

My grandfather left his family when my father was very young. My father was permitted to speak to his mother and grandparents, who basically raised him, in any tone of voice he wanted. He showed very little respect for them or their rules as he was growing up. When he became a parent, he decided that behavior was detrimental to a child, and resolved that it would be different in this family. As a result, displays of anger were not tolerated, and disagreements with him or my mother were discouraged. I learned to even monitor my facial expressions lest they be interpreted as disrespectful (my father seemed particularly sensitive to this). Unfortunately, I became very good at repressing anger. I developed an inability to say no, and I learned to plaster a pleasant look on my face no matter what. My parents, both coming from dysfunctional families, interpreted this just as most Adult Children trying to create a healthy family would. What they observed was a well-behaved, respectful, smiling child. It appeared that all was well with the world. Most Adult Children attempt to replicate something that they really don't understand and can get caught up in the outward appearance. Therapy in later years helped me incorporate the angry, assertive part of my self, to set limits, and to let go of needing everyone to love and approve of me.

## Non-Existent Boundaries

Establishing boundaries and setting limits on the part of the parent is an example of healthy modeling. These behaviors demonstrate taking care of oneself—an area of self-nurturing that our children need to see in action. Parenthood can be extremely exhausting if we do not allow ourselves some human limitations. Sometimes we allow our children to drain us of all our resources in subtle ways until one morning we wake up and find we have lost control of our lives.

How can this happen? Our mental programming may be delivering subconscious messages such as: *"To love is to sacrifice," "If I love you, I must give my all to you until there is nothing left for me,"* or *"Love means never having to say no."* These messages could originate from behaviors modeled to us in our own family. Perhaps our mother modeled this behavior by making sure everyone else had nice things while she went totally without. Perhaps one of our parents worked to the point of pure exhaustion so that we could have the "finer" things in life. These are admirable behaviors, but they set up detrimental prototypes for the children.

How do we as parents set boundaries or limits for ourselves? Consider the following questions:

1) Do you allow another family member to be verbally or physically abusive to you? Do you take on most of the responsibilities in the home?
2) Do you try to be all things to all of your children?
3) Are you unable to set limits for your children?
4) Are you unable to establish privacy so that you do not feel anxious while making love?
5) Are you unable take time for private moments or fun activities?

Affirmative answers to these questions indicate that you struggle to assert your needs. Being a parent does not negate being a person. Being a parent does not negate the fact that you have feelings, needs, and human limitations. Are you comfortable with the fact that you have human limitations?

It is important to set rules that will insure your privacy. Adults need privacy. Children need privacy too and we will examine this in the next chapter. Why are we afraid to say, "Knock on my bedroom door before entering, please," and enforce it? Why are we afraid to say, "I would like some uninterrupted time to read (sew, think, bathe, write)," and assert this? Why are we afraid to say, "Mommy and Daddy need some time alone," and insure this?

We need to set boundaries in other ways as well. When a family member is yelling, cursing, or treating us as if we belong under a rock, we need to say something like, "I will not continue this conversation until you can speak to me in a reasonable tone of voice."

There have been many times my own children (presently thirteen and eleven years old) pulled at me for more and more attention. Being a working mother, I try my best to give my children some quality attention in the evening. One activity that they enjoyed a few years ago was when I snuggled with them as they watched their favorite TV show. Unfortunately, this evening ritual became reminiscent of the tug-of-war games I used to play in elementary school. The only difference was that I had become the rope. One child would say, "Now it's my turn," and the other would reply, "No, she's only been with me for 10 minutes." There have been other times when I have felt like the baby the biblical King Solomon suggested slicing in half to pacify the two mothers. It is important for my children to know I feel this way—that I want to spend time with both of them and I am doing the best I can, but that I don't appreciate their lack of concern for my feelings as they argue over me like a piece of candy.

Being a parent does not negate having personal needs. There are times when we must assert our need for personal time, adult friends, work, and play. Although our children may experience some disappointment that we are taking time to be with someone other than them, or participating in an activity that doesn't involve them, they are learning a valuable lesson. They are learning that it must be OK to share us a little because in the end it is clear that we don't love them any less. Even though we don't spend every moment with them, being with them is still important to us. They learn this not because we tell them but because we *make* time for them. They are learning that life provides a variety of ways for people to fulfill their needs and express their love for self and others. They are learning that the world is not black and white but a blend of many components. Ultimately, they will fulfill their personal needs and assert their limits which will fulfill what we want for them.

If you have not been setting healthy boundaries in the past and decide to start, you may find yourself feeling guilty. Maybe that old tape is playing loud and clear: "Love means never having to say no."

It will take work to change it to: "Love means setting healthy examples from which my children can learn." As you institute changes in this area, be very consistent. Your children will test you. But if you are firm and consistent, the children will come to accept the changes.

If you find a mini-rebellion on your hands, take the time to verbalize the reasons for the change. This is a helpful approach when instituting any significant change in the family system. We don't want to repeat dysfunctional patterns such as keeping secrets and non-communication. Explain what you are learning about yourself at a level your children can understand. One possible approach might be, "When I have no time to do anything for myself, I feel more and more drained—like a flower that withers from lack of water. Would you rather be with a withered flower or a fresh one?"

## Overprotecting

If we find ourselves in that compulsive caretaker/rescuer role, or if we have assumed a basically fearful approach to life such as the Worrier, we are going to be key candidates for over-protecting our children.

Why is this undesirable? Our motivation is only to insure that our children don't experience pain of any sort—right?

Wrong. We cannot possibly be with each of our children every moment. What happens when we are not there? Instead of reaching inside and drawing on their own problem-solving experience, our children will be looking for a rescuer. They will have no other choice if they have not had the opportunity to problem solve for themselves.

A dear friend of mine would not allow her one-year-old son to topple when he was learning to walk. He was trying very hard to learn; it was Mom who was not letting it happen. She wanted him to walk but she did not want him to fall. Each time he would lean a little too far one way or the other, she would catch him and straighten him up.

He did not get an opportunity to learn: *OK, if I lean too far that way I'll fall so I don't want to do that.* He learned, *OK, if I lean too far in that direction I'll get to have fun when Mom catches me. She'll take care of me.* It's no wonder the child took a long time to walk. (He is now eleven-years-old and walking like a champ.)

Similarly, how does the child learn not to touch the stove and to respect heat? He will not know what the word *hot* means if we do not allow him to experience this at some safe level. Please notice that I added, "at some safe level." It is our responsibility to provide this basic learning in a way which does not endanger the child.

How else do we over-protect the child?

Eight-year-old Johnny forgets his homework assignment for the third time in the quarter. His mother has already received a notice that if this occurs again, his grade will be dropped one letter. He *begs* his mother to write a note to the teacher explaining that he was sick or that she accidentally threw out his homework. The mother, wishing to spare her son the ultimate consequence, complies.

This mother is behaving as an over-protective parent. She does not want her son's grade to drop, but which consequence is worse? A "C" instead of a "B" (or "D", or "E") in English, or a demonstrated lesson that it is no big deal to be irresponsible, and that someone will cover for you? The child will probably not be refused admission to college for getting a D in English in the third grade. But even if your high school student manipulates you in such a way, who is going to write that note for him when he does make it to college? Do you want him to grow up looking for people to write excuses for him? We can prevent this kind of behavior to a large degree and we will discuss this topic further in the next chapter.

## Living Vicariously—A Symptom of Enmeshment

There is a definite need to examine this issue in our parenting. It can profoundly affect the interaction with our children. When we have missed an opportunity in our own childhood or have trouble relinquishing certain childhood or adolescent activities in which we can no longer participate, there is a tendency to use our children to meet these needs.

Did you want to play baseball and never had the chance? Basketball? Football? Did you want to be a model, singer, or actress? What about a cheerleader, president of the Student Council, or Valedictorian? Most of us have had similar dreams. But how badly do you feel about missing these opportunities? Have you been able to let them go? Perhaps you were the football star, the captain of the cheerleaders, or a beautiful model. Have you been able to relinquish these roles as you move into a stage of life that is inconsistent with past self-images?

Most of us could probably think of at least one family where the parents did not get the opportunity to go to college because of financial reasons—but made sure their first-born became a college graduate. This may have worked out well if the child was similarly inclined—but it could be the disappointment of a lifetime if the child refuses to go or flunks out. These parents give themselves an "F" for parenthood based on this one "failure." The truth is that the child may have not have had the academic ability or perhaps dreamt of becoming an expert carpenter. Neither of these reasons for not going to college should be an indictment against parent or child. The fact that a child dreams a different dream has nothing to do with loving his parents any less.

If we pressure our children to play out our unfulfilled dreams, we run several risks. We may be setting up the child for failure by the fact that they will try to please us even if they don't have the skills, talent, interest, or potential. Do we want our child carrying this burden of guilt and inadequacy? *"I was a real disappointment to my parents." "I was never good enough to please them."* In addition, we send a dangerous message to our child when we pressure them to follow our dreams. *"My happiness is dependent on you. If you mess up your life (don't live it according to the gospel of me), then all of my dreams are lost."* This is an awesome burden for a child or adult to carry. It may sound extreme, but this kind of pressure is translated into similar messages by many children.

In my work with parents of chemically dependent adolescents, I have seen this dynamic played out over and over again. The mother says (his father just thinks it), "...but my son is my happiness. If he doesn't straighten out his life, I can't go on." The adolescent senses this. He is struggling with the disease of chemical dependency and cannot devote his full energy to recovery because there will be a double whammy if he fails. Not only will he destroy his own life, but his parents' as well. This burden is too much for an adolescent to handle. The responsibility for initial recovery alone could be compared to walking through life with a 100-pound weight on his shoulders. Now add the weight of being responsible for his parents' unhappiness and this boy is carrying around a 500-pound barbell. Will he be able to walk at all? Maybe the only way to deal with a weight that heavy is to medicate himself so he doesn't feel the weight.

What are the options for parents? We must release our own feelings of failure by realizing that we may no longer have control over our children after a certain age. This may be difficult to admit, particularly if we happen to be one of those adults who have control issues in the first place. I have found the following approaches helpful to parents in this position:

1. Give yourself credit for doing the best you could under the circumstances. You can hardly be guilty for not teaching something you have never learned.

Carol Koffinke

2. Some children choose a harder path to learn life's lessons. This does not necessarily mean that they will not reach the same goals as those who choose an easier path.

3. You pray that your children will have happy, fruitful lives, but you only have the control necessary to make your own life happy and fruitful.

The chemically-dependent adolescent, whose parents have reached the point of letting go of blame and responsibility, has been given two gifts. He may devote his full energy to recovery without the burden of additional guilt and shame for destroying his parents in the process. This will enhance the possibility for him to find recovery. Additionally, he will have a healthy, supportive system around him which shows that each of us has the responsibility to make our own lives happy. This is the *only* way any of us will achieve this goal. If I put all of my eggs in your basket, they will always be inaccessible to me and I have no control over whether or not you drop them.

The other side of vicarious living occurs when we have experienced something special that is gone but we can't seem to let it go. It is easy to think of examples of this. The mother who compulsively pushes her daughter into contests of popularity, beauty pageants, acting; the father who forces his son to play the sport in which he starred. This pressure to be whatever we want them to be will confuse their own attempts to find out who they are, what they like, what they want. Our children need to make these discoveries which will allow them to become responsible for their own happiness and to create fulfilling lives for themselves.

72

## Perfectionism

Even though we have already discussed the adult role of Perfectionist and will later examine the parental role, this characteristic deserves special consideration from all Adult Children. It is a form of compulsive behavior which demands attention if our children (and spouse) are to survive living with us. This is particularly true if we hope to take that a step further by actually having some sort of decent relationship with these people. Individuals who require their outside world to be in perfect shape are usually struggling with an inside world that is confused, afraid, and are grasping at straws to make some sense out of life. You will seldom, if ever, meet a person who expects everyone else to be perfect while they are totally lackadaisical about themselves. Likewise, it is extremely rare for an individual to be "perfect" while accepting a more relaxed approach from others.

This perfectionism may be manifested in a variety of ways. There may be a compulsive need for timeliness. These individuals become very agitated when others do not respect the clock the way they do. They are particularly distraught when they are prevented from being on time.

Extreme neatness can be another form of perfectionism. Clothes must be perfectly pressed and each hair must be in place. These individuals' homes must be picked up at all times, and if they do not live alone, demands are placed on others (often in the form of nagging) to insure their standards are met. Others are expected to have the same sense of pride in their appearance, and to share the same definition of attractiveness. There is often a residual anger when others relax even in their own room, don't constantly pick up after themselves, or fail to routinely perform "dirt patrol."

"A job worth doing is worth doing well." "Cleanliness is next to Godliness." "A place for everything and everything in its place." These are the types of messages that can turn life into a rigid washboard as the perfectionist painfully scrubs against other people's lack of cooperation with their values.

To live with a perfectionist can be very oppressive. One must become hypervigilant or numb. Perfectionists expect everyone to see the world through their eyes but are unable to do the same. Family members find themselves constantly nagged to do things differently (like the perfectionist). They can either sit on the edge of their chair when they are around so that their behavior is not "wrong," or they can tune the person out. Either way, the family member is distancing themselves from the perfectionist. Why would they want to connect with a person who can only see what they do wrong?

If we have perfectionistic tendencies, we should lighten up on ourselves. If we can forgive ourselves and accept our own humanness, we can begin the process of smoothing out the washboard ridges. Once we allow ourselves some flexibility, we can allow others the same. But because the perfectionism which is focused outward is a projection of our internal process, the work must start inside—in our relationship with ourselves.

### Rigidity

This characteristic spills over from our discussion of perfectionism. But it deserves some separate attention because there are areas of rigidity which do not apply to perfectionism. Examples are with rules, routines, and attitudes.

I have experienced some difficulties with rigidity myself. One message I had programmed from my family was *Good mothers cook a dinner for the family each evening to include a meat, vegetable and starch.* When I was growing up this message was as consistent as the sun rising in the morning. My mother never *told* me that this was the rule, but since she accomplished this feat every evening, I registered it as the standard. My mother did not work outside the home. This goal seemed to be reasonable. Even though I have almost always held a full-time job, I still felt compelled to perform this ritual of consistent, healthy family dinners every evening. After work, I would walk through the door and turn on the oven before I had even removed my coat. There would be no time for interaction with children while I frantically scrambled to get a full meal on the table at an hour that wouldn't cause clean up to go into the next day. This hour became such a nightmare for me, I decided I was being unreasonable. So, I loosened up the standard a bit. (I hit bottom regarding this issue the night I threw a salami sandwich with a carrot stick on my children's plate and said, "There—meat, vegetable, starch." See what I mean by overcompensating?). Now I cook a full meal when I can: I don't when I can't. But I still feel guilty sometimes.

As this example illustrates, rigidity is an inability to be flexible or bend with circumstances. It keeps a person locked into rules, often derived from the past, which no longer work. Rigidity prevents us from taking into account what is happening at the moment and making the appropriate decisions. Most of all, rigidity keeps us from operating effectively in situations and relating effectively with people.

Rigidity can also lead to resentment. We sometimes find ourselves strapped to a sinking ship. It can cause our child to resent us as we refuse to listen to their point of view because, "This is they way things are."

Consider these questions:

1) Do you have difficulty relaxing a rule once in a while?
2) Do others accuse you of not listening and considering their point of view?
3) Would you resist interrupting a routine to take advantage of a spontaneous opportunity?
4) Do you struggle with modifying standards even when the circumstances call for some flexibility?

Affirmative answers indicate a tendency toward rigidity.

Changing rigidity may be difficult because it is one way we try to create security for ourselves. This characteristic is often well-developed in Adult Children and may require outside help to change. When we can be flexible, we teach our children to bend in the wind rather than break. This is another gift we can give our children.

Chapter Six

# You The Parent

We now come upon a crucial point in our journey. Who are we as parents and what legacies are we passing on to our children? Have we been able to effectively change what we know in our hearts needs to be changed or are we simply passing on the same painful lessons that we learned and were unable to denounce? Perhaps we have even fooled ourselves into believing that we have changed the legacy when in fact we have only altered the form in which it has been bestowed.

I will begin this chapter by telling you a secret.

**Most parents have totally overlooked the most powerful tool they possess in shaping their child's development and personality!**

For this reason, we will start this leg of our journey by learning about this potent ally.

## Modeling

Sometimes, the situations that we want to change (and probably should change) in our own families are met with great inner resistance. In certain ways, we want to act differently from our parents. But we become astounded when we suddenly hear ourselves using a tone of voice we hated, or speaking a line that would make our skin crawl. We may glance in the mirror and observe an expression that reminds us so much of a parent that we become momentarily immobilized.

Modeling is a powerful learning tool. We see this over and over in the chemically dependent family where the child says, "It will never happen to me." ACOA's propensity to make this statement is so common that Claudia Black wrote a book entitled, *It Will Never Happen To Me*. When modeled by a parent, chemically dependent behavior has a powerful effect on the child's ability to live a chemically-free life, not discounting the genetic aspect of this disease. The child does not want to become an alcoholic or addict. Yet most do drink or use drugs which allows their disease to develop.

Another common example which illustrates the power of modeling is the physically abused child. As Adult Children these individuals cannot wait to have their own baby to show it the love, tenderness and affection that they never had. Yet when they experience the frustration of parenthood, they abuse the child—the child they brought into the world to save. Why? Because that is how they were taught to deal with frustration and anger. They most likely were not told to hit someone when they felt this way. They *saw* that this was how to deal with these feelings. All the coaxing in the world from a parent to teach them to express their frustration appropriately would have been meaningless if at the same time they watched their parents strike out at them or others under similar circumstances.

I have worked with many co-dependents who want such wonderful lives for their children. All of them wish for that fairy godmother who would grant their offspring happiness, health, wealth, and love.

Yet, as parents, many grew up in homes where healthy modeling was absent. It becomes difficult to learn how to go about this. The parent who is struggling with co-dependent issues will find it difficult to set a healthy example of how to be happy. We have already seen in previous chapters that co-dependents are plagued by compulsive behaviors, repressed feelings, and an insatiable need for outside validation. Mistakenly, they think children will learn to be happy because they wish it to be so.

*"I want my child to feel good about himself."* Yet the parents repeatedly model putting their own needs last, compromising themselves for others, putting out energy for everyone but themselves. How will the children learn that it's all right to nurture themselves, that their needs are as important as anyone else's, that they too have rights?

It is not fruitful for parents to make the child's needs more important than their own. By insuring that all our children's needs are gratified, we hope to teach them that their needs are important. What we really teach, however, is *"Someone else will take care of your needs,"* which encourages dependency in adult relationships. If we have neglected our own needs in this process, the message additionally becomes: *"I have sacrificed my needs for yours because that's what love is all about."* This establishes a prototype for caretaking behaviors on the part of our children. There is no opportunity for the child to observe an adult who takes responsibility for his or her own happiness. As long as any of us are dependent on someone other than ourselves for fulfillment, we are searching for the way home down a dead end street. We need to show our children that it is permissible for Mom and Dad to have their needs met too. Believe it or not that will encourage them much more to place their own needs in position of importance than watching the parent become worn down as he or she tries to be everything to everyone else. Without healthy modeling, the imprinting will exist. When the child becomes involved in a love relationship, the mental programming will play out: *"I am willing to sacrifice my needs for yours because I love you."*

The pendulum can swing too much in the opposite direction as well. I have worked with many recovering co-dependents who have gone from compulsive caretaking to refusing to help a four-year-old tie his shoes. The healthy solution is a balance of both. *"I need to take care of myself, but I an secure enough in this area that I can temporarily put my needs aside to help you."*

We don't want our children to be dependent or caretaking in their relationships as adults. We hope to see them in satisfying, nurturing relationships. We pray that they become mature, responsible adults. We yearn to give them every opportunity to make a life for themselves that is fulfilling, creative, and enriched with positive experiences. How can we go about this?

There is no magical recipe. The most powerful way is to allow our children the opportunity to learn these lessons by observing them. When they see us securing time for ourselves, it gives them permission to do the same. When they observe us taking time out for fun, they can learn this is an important activity for adults. When they see us saying "no," they will set limits and disagree with others.

Emotional health is another gift we would give our children if we could. As we have observed in this section on Modeling, the best way to give this gift is to *be* this gift. This means allowing ourselves to appropriately express the *full* range of feelings, not only the "good ones." Children will experience the full range of emotions because they are human beings just like us. This includes anger, hurt, fear, guilt, embarrassment, sadness, and shame as well as happiness, love, compassion, and elation. If we attempt to protect them from experiencing negative feelings by denying their existence within ourselves, we teach our children that these feelings are not OK. This sets up an early pattern of denial and repression which they observe and internalize into their mental and emotional programming. The devastating effects of this kind of behavior were reviewed in Chapters Two and Three.

Let's look at an example. When Mom is having a bad day, her children can sense it. They are very apt to ask her what is wrong, especially since they are probably experiencing a nagging sensation that whatever is wrong has something to do with them. (This response is fairly typical as children believe they are the center of the world and thus have tremendous power to influence it.) If she responds, "Nothing," the children may draw one or more of the following conclusions:

- Mom isn't always truthful with me (actions and words are inconsistent).
- It must not be OK to have a bad day since she is obviously trying to hide it.
- I must have done something but she just won't tell me. (child keeps a vague feeling of guilt until our mood changes.)

Let's replay this simple scene differently. When the children asked Mom what was wrong, she might have replied, "I'm having a bad day today. That happens sometimes but it has nothing to do with you." The children would have an opportunity to learn the following lessons:

- Mom gives me honest answers when I ask,
- It must be OK to not feel great all the time—she admitted to feeling that way.
- Whatever is wrong has nothing to do with me (gives child permission to go about the business of being a child).

Somewhere down the line when the child experiences a bad day, part of him will tap into this sort of program. They will subconsciously retrieve, *"Mom survived this, I guess I will too."* The moods which are a normal part of the maturation process will seem much less powerful to them simply because they are aware that a parent has experienced the same feelings as well as having had the opportunity to observe that they don't last forever.

We tend to set up superhuman standards for our children. This is inadvertently accomplished by denying our humanness, trying to hide our humanness, or trying to be all things to all people. These kinds of behaviors can cause our children to fear adulthood. They fear they can't measure up, that adulthood is an awesome responsibility. They feel inadequate as they naturally fail at the task of being godlike. It is much better to share with our children the secret that we are real human beings. We are, in fact, persons who can have bad days and recuperate, who can survive negative feelings, and who can make a mistake and learn. We are, in fact, persons who may appear "big" but who are still growing with life's experiences. They won't love us any less for it and this offers an attainable goal for our children.

Are you accepting of your own humanness?

## Parenting Roles

Now that you understand the concept of modeling and its ability to support or negate what you teach your children, we will move forward. Our approach to the world has developed through our experiences. These experiences determine how we deal with emotions and life, and is incorporated into our parenting approach. Each adult role presented in Chapter Four contains certain parenting traps inherent in the related issues. You most likely identified with at least one of these behavior types and can gain some parenting insights as you review them again with this focus. The questions after each section are meant to assist you in becoming aware of particular parenting traps associated with each role.

## Overachiever/People-Pleaser

Because this individual is very performance- oriented, there is often much pressure put on the children to meet very high standards. This parent's identity is still tied to personal achievement which is often projected onto the children. The subconscious thought process is: *My identity is tied to your achievements because my identity is tied to my achievements and you are an extension of me.* The dynamic of enmeshment, examined in the last chapter, is common in this role as well as any untreated Adult Child parenting roles.

These parents tend to take life very seriously. They may be impatient and uncooperative in regards to their child's need to play and act like a child. They themselves most likely held the role of miniature adult at the same age.

The people-pleasing side models outer focused behavior. When pleasing others is a priority, parents will have difficulty validating their child's need to assert himself or disagree with others. Without the permission to speak up, their child will fall into the same trap that they themselves fell into in their own family. *My thoughts, feelings, and needs are not as important as someone else's, therefore I am not as important as someone else.*

One other point about this adult role in parenthood needs to be examined. The Overachiever/People- Pleaser has difficulty accepting his humanness. He has difficulty acknowledging mistakes and forgiving himself for not being perfect. Modeling this harsh self-criticism teaches the children that mistakes are not OK. This could set them up for failure in adulthood.

Consider the following questions:

1) Do you have difficulty allowing your children to act silly and frivolous at times?
2) Do you resist playing with them?
3) Do you think you pressure rather than encourage your children to excel?

4) Do you feel a sense of shame when they do not do well in school or in a particular activity that you have encouraged?

5) Do you encourage your children to do whatever is necessary to keep the peace at home and in the outside world?

6) Do you have difficulty validating your child when he makes mistakes?  Do you overreact?

These questions indicate issues for the parent who identifies with the Overachiever/People-Pleaser. Now that these issues have been identified, you can begin to work on them.

### Perfectionist

This parental role is similar to the Overachiever except that these individuals direct their criticism more toward others rather than toward themselves.  This parent is seldom satisfied with his child's performance, behavior, and appearance.  If the child gets good grades, he is getting too fat.  If he has lost weight, he needs to get his skin cleared up.  If he is mowing the lawn in rows, he should be mowing it in squares.  The child will become frustrated with trying to please the parent and may develop a sense of inadequacy that nothing he can do will ever be good enough.  This type of behavior on the part of the parent alienates the child who will have a tendency to avoid the criticism.

Consider these questions:

1) Are you sometimes accused of being too critical of your children?

2) Do you find it difficult to refrain from criticizing or directing your child to do something differently even when you know the timing is bad?

3) Do you want to improve the way your child does simple things like coloring a picture, playing with a toy, making a sandwich?
4) Have you been accused of being a nag?
5) Do your children seem to be avoiding contact with you?

These questions indicate issues for the parent who identifies with the Perfectionist. Now that these issues have been identified, you can begin to work on them.

### Controller

As we have seen earlier, these individuals have a compulsive need to control and tend to do so in repressive kinds of ways. As a parent they will use intimidation and guilt to insure they get their way.

This type of parent models several unhealthy behaviors for his children. *"It's going to be my way."* The child can't overtly win with this parent but this message will still be incorporated into his learning. The child therefore develops methods where he can manipulate at least some things to be *his* way (just as his parent made it his way) such as developing an eating disorder or rebelling. It becomes obvious to the child on some level that another message is: *"I must control you to maintain a sense of power for myself."* The child may find himself acting this message out in similar ways with peers by becoming a bully or "tough guy."

These parents may prevent their children from learning how to make decisions for themselves since giving up that control challenges the parents' power play. As we will see in the next chapter, decision-making is a necessary skill in the development of self-confidence.
Consider these questions:

1) Do you find yourself unable to listen to your child's point of view when it comes to making a decision that involves him or her?

2) Do you experience anxiety when challenged by your child?
3) Do you intimidate your children when you sense they may be resistant to what you want?
4) Do you resort to making them feel guilty when they don't fully cooperate with you?

These questions indicate issues for the parent who identifies with the Controller. Now that these issues have been identified, you can begin to work on them.

## Caretaker

As parents these individuals overprotect their children in an attempt to assure that they do not experience pain or discomfort. We see this in the parent who writes the false note to the teacher so that the child who doesn't complete his homework escapes any negative consequence. This type of parent will rescue the child from any kind of natural consequence.

Doing for children what they can do for themselves results in many missed opportunities for the child to learn the necessary lessons of life and to mature developmentally. This parent (not out of desire but out of unresolved issues) may produce offspring who are unmotivated, irresponsible, and immature because of the lack of opportunities to deal with age appropriate life issues. Caretakers model that one should take care of others and not oneself—even though they may wish with all of their heart that the children grow into healthy, productive individuals.

If this parent is so involved in caretaking neighbors and friends, there may be a lack of time and energy available for quality parenting. Often the biggest drain on the parent is not the cooking or keeping the house together. It is dealing with negative emotions, behavior, and problems. This parent may avoid these kinds of issues.

Consider these questions:

1) Do you have difficulty following through on expectations communicated to your children such as making their beds, cleaning their room, helping around the house?
2) Do you find yourself rescuing them from natural consequences such as failure to do homework, or lying to get them out of some sort of trouble?
3) Do you find yourself frequently on the phone or out of the house helping others?

These questions indicate issues for the parent who identifies with the Caretaker. Now that these issues have been identified, you can begin to work on them.

## Rebel

As we have seen, this is an angry individual. As a parent, the Rebel creates an angry atmosphere in the family. Anger may be directed toward spouse or children or both, but it can become the chronic stress producer as other family members modify themselves accordingly to minimize the attacks. Children from this family learn fear well. Some of these children will incorporate this angry behavior. They will see it as a way to hide their fear and to gain power and control over siblings and peers. Thus, the bully is born.

There are definite similarities between the Controller and the Rebel except that the Rebel may not be motivated toward anger by someone not doing something his way. Rebels struggle with anger and may manufacture a situation which will provide them a vehicle for expression. Thus, we see the parent who changes the rules without telling anybody or who appears to be satisfied with a child's behavior or appearance one day, but is enraged over it the next.

Because this individual tends to marry someone who is passive and has problems asserting his or her own needs, the children may model themselves after the passive parent since it seems the best way to keep the peace. Either extreme, passivity or aggression, is not a behavior which will serve the children well in their own development as individuals.

Consider these questions:

1) Do you frequently yell at your children?
2) Do you sometimes use them as a scapegoat when you know that what you are really angry about has nothing to do with them?
3) Do you think your children are afraid of you?
4) Do you hate to be challenged by your children?

These questions indicate issues for the parent who identifies with the Rebel. Now that these issues have been identified, you can begin to work on them.

### Doormat

These adults have difficulty asserting themselves and expressing their needs. This parent models to the children that it's not OK to take care of yourself. If the role is played by the mother, the daughter learns that men are strong, women are weak, and that men's needs are more important than women's. The son has little opportunity to learn respect for the opposite sex as being worthwhile human beings. If the father is the Doormat, the daughter learns that power comes from controlling men even if she is angry at her mother for always having the upper hand. She, like the son in the previous situation, does not get an opportunity to develop a feeling of respect for the opposite sex. The son in this case may experience anger toward Mom for *"Walking all over Dad"* and may try to rebel to assert his need to be a man. He may develop an underlying hate for women since he may believe that his mother was responsible for emasculating his father. It is possible that he will follow the role model himself and become the Doormat but there are many cultural teachings that may influence him otherwise. Common sayings that preach male dominance are: *Who wears the pants in the family? What, are you, henpecked? He's doesn't have the balls (not strong or brave enough)!*

This parent usually avoids conflict and will have difficulty following through on boundaries and rules set for the children. The children will see that this parent won't "stick to his or her guns" and they will test more frequently than children who have the rules clearly defined. This situation is also ripe for manipulation on the part of the children. If they can't get their way with the other parent, they will try to get it with this one. They may be successful with this unless the Doormat is more afraid of the spouse than the children.

Consider the following questions:

1) Do you avoid conflict with your children as much as possible?
2) Are you sometimes ignored by your children when making a request to have something done?
3) Do your children get angry at your spouse for "walking all over you?"
4) Do you feel discounted in the family?

These questions indicate issues for the parent who identifies with the Doormat. Now that these issues have been identified, you can begin to work on them.

## Entertainer

The most prominent parenting trap for this individual is that he will have difficulty taking their children's problems seriously. This may sound minor, but it can significantly inhibit the willingness of the children to communicate and receive the help they need to work through whatever catastrophe they are encountering at the time. Regardless of the child's age, he or she will experience difficulties that to an adult may seem quite trivial. To the children, however, it could mean feeling like the world is coming to an end. A parent who is unable to listen to their child's troubles may alienate the child.

Like most untreated Adult Children, these parents have difficulty relating to their children on a feeling level. When they are having a bad day, or feeling disappointed about something, they will lie when their child asks, "What's wrong?" This teaches the child that it is not OK to feel upset or sad. When the child does feel upset or sad, he will think something is wrong with him that he can't be happy-go-lucky like Mommy or Daddy all of the time. Some children will react to the comic front with some anger. Deep down they know that the joking stands in the way of themselves and their parent. It is the wall between a self-to-self connection. As a result, they may feel resentful and lonely.

Consider these questions:

1) Do you feel obligated to keep your children's spirits up?
2) Do you often discount their problems as simple "molehills"?
3) Are you unable to share feelings with your children such as sadness, disappointment, and irritability?
4) Do you receive criticism from your children about joking around all of the time?

These questions indicate issues for the parent who identifies with the Entertainer. Now that these issues have been identified, you can begin to work on them.

## Baby

When these Adult Children encounter parenthood, one of two things will happen. They may be abruptly snapped into the reality that the Baby role can't possibly work for them in this situation and decide to work on themselves. Or, they may decide to fight for their Baby turf despite the addition of a third party. If the parent remains the Baby, the children—especially the older ones—may end up joining the ranks of those who care for him. The youngest is most likely to model the Baby behavior. It follows the birth order rule of thumb. The older children become Caretakers and the youngest becomes the Baby.

This parent also has difficulty being there emotionally for his children. Parenthood is an awesome responsibility, and this Baby will avoid getting too involved if at all possible.

Consider these questions:

1) Do you sometimes feel jealous when your children get too much attention from your spouse?
2) Do you feel threatened by the responsibility of being a parent?
3) Do your children seem to do things for you that a parent would most likely do for a child, such as fixing your meals, reminding you of important events, and waiting on you?
4) Do you resent having to bring home a pay check?

These questions indicate issues for the parent who identifies with the Baby. Now that these issues have been identified, you can begin to work on them.

## Worrier

Children create very fertile ground for the Worrier. This parent will nag and overprotect the children. This parent communicates clearly that the world is not to be trusted. Most likely, the children will not stretch their wings—which they must do if they want to fly as adults. Imagine a mother robin unwilling to allow her fledglings to venture too close to the edge of the nest. This is the effect the Worrier can have on the child. A child will only learn his own safe boundaries by being allowed to explore, touch, and peek over them. These lessons cannot be merely verbally taught. They must be experienced by the one who is growing.

As children attempt to spread their wings, the trauma to the Worrier may be so severe that the children can become guilt ridden. "How could you do this to me?" the Worrier cries when the child is late for dinner. "I have spent one entire hour knowing, just knowing, that you were kidnapped. Where *were* you?"

It is possible that the Worrier may focus fear elsewhere, as well as on the children. In these cases the children often become surrogate mothers as they attempt to assure the Worrier that he or she doesn't need to be so upset. Everything will be all right.

Consider these questions:

1) Do you often seem to worry about situations that end up working out OK?
2) Do you feel most other parents are insensitive to the possible traumas that await their children?
3) Do you tend to get worked up about things and end up being soothed by your children?
4) Have you been accused by others of being overprotective of your children?

These preceding questions indicate issues for the parent who identifies with the Worrier. Now that these issues have been identified, you can begin to work on them.

By now you probably have a strong sense of issues in your adult and parent roles that may need attention. Good. That is more than half the battle. In the next chapter we will look at your children and how these issues play into your relationship with them. You will also learn some fundamental approaches which will assist you in exerting a positive influence over their development.

Change does not occur overnight. If you have identified certain personal characteristics or behaviors you wish to modify, great! It is very important, however, to be patient and gentle with yourself. A sizeable span lies between an old behavior and a new one with many intermediate steps in between. There will be slips and the acting out of old scripts from the past. That is to be expected as we try and initiate change. Becoming the best parents we can be requires redefining what healthy parenting means for us as we learn more and more about ourselves and the patterns passed on from one generation to the next.

Also remember that becoming positive, supportive, loving parents does not mean that our children will turn out "perfectly" (which of course would be defined differently from parent to parent). Children have to experience life firsthand at some point. This means making mistakes and learning from them. As we model healthy adulthood, however, we help supply them with the tools to survive life's normal ups and downs and to grow in the process. We can step back knowing that we did our best to love and teach our children what we could. The rest is up to them.

Chapter Seven

# Your Children:
# What And How To Give

As loving parents, we all want good things for our children. Most of us—especially if we are the product of a dysfunctional family system, need to be taught how to give the gifts inside of us. This section will focus more on the child and our interaction with them. We will explore how to nurture certain traits essential for the development of adults who can be responsible for making their own life a happy, fulfilling one. We will also look at our children as individuals who have different needs rather than perpetuating the message: *What goes for one, goes for all.* This announces, *I treat my children all the same,* which, of course, means no one is special. Our children are special, and need to know it.

Let us examine several qualities that can benefit our children beyond words. *Self-esteem* provides a stable foundation from which a person may grow, and a safe, personal haven for retreat. It gives a person permission to care for self and others and to act accordingly. *Self-confidence* provides the motivation and security to reach beyond one's safely established boundaries and establish new goals. It promotes the stretching of the wings to explore the unknown. *A Sense of Responsibility* supplies the muscle that pushes a person to achieve those new goals and to deal effectively with the realities of life. *Discipline* strengthens that muscle so that the work can be done. Maybe the effort involves making a marriage good, or changing what a person needs to change so they can become a healthy parent. Maybe the work involves becoming a good artist or skillful brain surgeon.

Most parents desire their children to possess such qualities. Let us consider them individually and explore how to nurture their development.

## Self-Esteem

When we value and respect ourselves, a positive reality is created which will manifest itself in all areas of our lives: *"We are worthwhile; we deserve a good life."* There is a logical reason for this. Feeling good about ourselves and accepting ourselves for who we are motivates us to take proper care of ourselves. Look at how differently one might treat a valuable heirloom pin as opposed to one bought in the Five-and-Dime Store. Which do you suppose will be placed in a velvet case and polished regularly?

When our children value themselves, their decisions will be beneficial, not harmful. Self-esteem establishes a protective coating between them and such things as peer pressure. Thus the power of outside pressure is diminished and they are less vulnerable to harmful influences.

High self-esteem positively influences the kinds of relationships our child will choose. If I value my pin, I will not let someone who I do not trust wear it. If I do lend it out, I will expect that person to treat it well.

Our children need to respect themselves and to feel that they are worthwhile individuals. This is one aspect of our child's development where we as parents can have a tremendous impact. Children look to us for their own self-worth. If they know we love them, they believe they are lovable. If they believe they are lovable, they are beginning to form a foundation for healthy self-esteem. Loving our children with all of our hearts does not mean that we successfully communicate that love to them. We must learn how to communicate this love. All the good intentions and warm affection in the world will be for naught if we are unable to let them feel the love. If, as a parent, our own self-esteem is located somewhere in the dregs of a pond, this task of communicating love to our children becomes much more difficult. This personal lack will cause us to extract feelings of self-worth from our children, much like the child seeks to extract these feelings from the parent. If this is the case, we will end up taking much more from our children than we give (see Chapter Four, *Injured Child*). Counseling may be helpful in overcoming this obstacle to healthy parenting.

•Unconditional Love•

How do we help our children know that we love them? There is a concept called unconditional love which sets the stage for this communication. This concept indicates the highest form of love. We are able to love our children no matter what they do or say. Loving unconditionally includes a responsibility to help them understand that we can be angry with them and still love them. It is a constant which exists even through situations where disappointment, anger, and consequences are involved. This kind of love transforms us into a permanent safety net for our children, no matter what they experience. They know that no matter how badly they mess up, there still exists someone in the world who loves and accepts them. Because unconditional love is not dependent on outside influences such as appearance, performance and behavior, we can keep from being sucked into their world—a world that often seems to be disintegrating around them. They need their safety net supporting them at a distance.

## •Touch•

We also need to communicate this love by touch. This aspect of loving is much more difficult for some to express than others—and the reason for this is not always easily understood. Still, most children yearn to be touched by their parents. There is no set way to do it. Showing affection between parent and child includes many possibilities: hugging, kissing, holding on a lap, scratching a back, patting and rubbing. A firm handshake or brief pat on the back, however, does *not* qualify. The attempt at affection needs to last at least long enough for a warmth from the parent to be communicated.

For those who are very uncomfortable expressing affection to the child, attempts may feel very clumsy. The firm handshake given to the eight-year-old for a game well-played is an awkward attempt to express pride in the child. How lovely if all parents could give affection to their children freely and spontaneously. But old scripts can prevent this. Fear of showing the soft side and unresolved trust issues (Rebel) can prevent a parent from showing affection. Fear of getting too close (Loner) also may hinder the freedom of spontaneous affection toward children.

There are phases when a child is less accepting of love from a parent. These phases will normally correspond to a stage in the child's development and his attempt to establish a sense of autonomy appropriate to his age level. It is not appropriate for a ten-year-old boy to establish his independence by moving out of the house. It is appropriate for him to request that his mother not kiss him in front of the "boys."

My son has always been a very affectionate child, both on the giving and receiving ends. It was something I almost felt smug about when I heard other mothers discuss how their sons resisted their affection after a certain age. I hope I didn't communicate that smugness to any other mothers who were around the day I took my eight-year-old son to his football game. We got out of the car and I tried to walk with my arm around his shoulder. Not only did he shy away from my touch, but he gave the following instructions to me under his breath, "Mom, how about walking back about ten feet?"

• Shame On You •

Let's examine two scenes which illustrate a disciplinary technique used by many parents.

A small child picks up Mom's favorite candy dish and accidentally drops and breaks it. Mom is angry and she says, "Shame on you for breaking Mommy's pretty dish." The intent is to change the child's behavior by creating feelings of guilt and shame.

> Problem #1. It was an accident and we cannot prevent children from having them.
>
> Problem #2. The child most likely feels badly anyway knowing she did something wrong.
>
> Problem #3. She is being taught that to be *wrong* is to be *bad*—a lesson that is programmed.

A seven-year-old boy occasionally wets the bed. Mom says, "Shame on you. You're too old for this." The intent is to make him feel ashamed so that he won't do it again.

> Problem #1. The normal seven-year-old boy does not *want* to wet the bed. So why are we trying to convince him not to do it?
>
> Problem #2. We are teaching him that he is bad because he did something that he couldn't help and probably didn't even know he was doing until sometime after it occurred.
>
> Problem #3. Creating feelings of guilt and shame will only worsen this problem.

Many of us probably experienced in our own family the behavior modification technique of "Shame on you." In an attempt to control us, our parents may have utilized a variety of approaches to include causing a feeling of shame to surface if we did something wrong. As parents ourselves, we are anxious for our children to "mind" us. And so we employ whatever techniques we feel may work.

There are so many ways we play "Shame on you." Creating a feeling of shame in a child convinces him that at least part of his basic nature is bad. Since the message is delivered by the omnipotent parent, the child will be more likely to accept this as his basic nature rather than to try to change it. One reason is because he wouldn't have the slightest idea of how to begin. Also, we, the powerful parents, are the ones reflecting back to the child what we see. *This is how I see you—bad, bad, bad.* The young child accepts the world that we allow him to experience as reality because there is no other. There will be little energy on his part to change the outward behavior because most energy will be going inward to deal with the emotional pain of being *bad, bad, bad.* So, this teaching is fairly ineffective in changing behavior and also results in low self-esteem for our children.

When I reprimand my son, he asks for validation of my love. "Mommy, do you still love me?" I try to take this opportunity to teach him something about unconditional love. It has *nothing at all* to do with anger or making mistakes.

"I can love you and still be angry with what you did," I tell him. "Love is permanent. I'm angry about what happened today. (Child learns: Anger must be OK. She still loves me.) You made a mistake. Everyone makes mistakes. You can never do anything bad enough to make me stop loving you." (Child learns: I can't be too bad, she still loves me.)

Did you react to these responses with a vague sense of fear that you will be giving your children carte blanche to behave badly or to make you angry? The better they feel about themselves, the more capable they will be of making *constructive* choices—like the heirloom pin. If they value themselves, they will put themselves away in the velvet-lined box and shine themselves regularly. This means constructive, not destructive behavior.

If you identified at all with the Perfectionist (overly critical) parent in chapter Six, take a moment to think about the impact these traits can have on the children. Their sense of self-esteem will be affected if they believe that they never do anything right. Our definition of "right" needs to encompass more than having things done "our way." We need to stop picking at every little thing they do. A child *will not* do things as well as an adult. At the same time we have a responsibility to be honest if they are to learn. Finding this happy medium will take some practice. But understanding how to correct our children without shaming them will help.

Here are some examples:

ITEM:  Posture.
      Negative:  You look like an old lady.  Stand up straight!
      Positive:  You look much prettier when you stand straight.
           Here, look in the mirror.

ITEM:  Chore performed unsatisfactorily.
      Negative:  What do you think we are?  Pigs?  Do it again!
      Positive:  It looks like you rushed through this.  Try it again.

ITEM:  Too much make-up/weird clothes
      Negative:  You look like a slut!  Go wash your face.
      Positive:  I don't think that's appropriate for school.
           Please take it off.

The difference between the negative and the positive is the difference between attacking the child and teaching him. If attacked, the child will direct his energy into healing his wounds, not into learning.

## Self-Confidence

Another characteristic that is important for us to nurture in our children is self-confidence. We cannot be with them every moment of their lives—even as children. They play with friends, go to school, and eventually leave home (if all goes well). Therefore, it is not enough that we take good care of them and protect them from harm. They must learn how to do this for themselves.

What are the desirable qualities of this trait? A person who is self-confident has the ability to make sound decisions and to take appropriate risks. Fortunately, we as parents have a great deal of molding power in regard to these skills. If we nurture the development of these abilities, they emerge and blossom. If we smother them, they never see the light of day.

How to nurture self-confidence in our children varies at the different stages of development. We don't need to be child psychologists to understand or accomplish this task. We probably miss the everyday opportunities to let them experiment with decision-making or taking risks just because we really have not incorporated this skill into our parenting awareness.

### •Decision-Making•

Allowing children to make choices for themselves is something we can encourage at a very young age, keeping in mind the child's limitations. It is not appropriate to allow a three-or four-year-old the option of whether or not to go to bed, take a bath, or mind Mom or Dad. Allowing him or her to make decisions means accepting the choices they make. I would not be willing to accept the alternatives in these areas. However, we can let them experiment in areas such as choosing what to wear. Narrowing down the options is important for younger children so that they are not overwhelmed or end up wearing a wool sweater in July. Lay out two appropriate outfits and let your child choose. This tiny venture encourages him to think about their own likes and dislikes. It allows them to experience a tiny moment of independence *(Mom won't make every decision for me)*, and to feel good about himself if his choice is validated. The developmental process involves a passage from dependence to healthy autonomy. Presenting these kinds of opportunities can help children along the way.

Dinner time presents another opportunity to help the young child experience decision-making. From the age of four or so I allowed my children to make the decision to either finish their dinner or not have dessert. I was careful not to put too much food on their plates. If they asked whether or not they had to eat it all, I would merely say, "No, you can choose to either finish your dinner and have dessert, or you may get down. But there will be no dessert or sweets this evening." It was amazing to see how seriously they considered these choices. They seemed to envision the evening without a snack and usually finished their meal. Again, I did not pile up their plate. But I expected that protein and vegetable would be consumed if any sweets were to follow. I have never had a dinner battle with either of my children and they are both good eaters and have no weight problems.

This situation allowed them two opportunities: (1) to make a decision for which they would be totally responsible and which had consequences attached, and (2) to learn a little more about making the best choice.

If children are able to gain confidence in their ability to make decisions at an early age, they will be less susceptible to peer pressure when they are adolescents. Children who value themselves and have already experienced a series of decision-making opportunities are less likely to fall prey to the power of a group or another person. If they have a stored program which validates that they have made and are capable of making sound decisions, they will be able to use that ability in situations, for example, where they are pressured to use drugs. They know who they are, they know what is good for them, and they have developed enough independence to make the best choice. If Mom or Dad has been making all of the decisions for them up to that point, they will be more likely to allow the other person to make the decision for them.

Here are examples of other opportunities for teaching decision-making:

Recreation—movies or park?

What time to take a shower.

What pet to choose.

What game Dad or Mom will play with them.

What toy to choose in the store.

What time a chore is to be done.

### •Encouragement•

Parents can influence how children program experiences of success and failure into their mental/emotional computers. If we place a shoe on a three-year-old and expect him to tie it well, the child experiences an early lesson in not meeting Mom or Dad's expectations. It is better to break down tasks and allow the child to try something he is capable of accomplishing. The task might consist of only the first step of the shoe-tying process, or cutting a soft carrot (as opposed to steak), or matching socks in the laundry (not folding sweaters). When the child experiences success, we can challenge him further. They need to feel confident in their ability to succeed if they are to attempt new tasks. Would you try to compose a symphony before you could write a song?

We can help our children build their self-confidence by praising them on even small successes. This small effort on our part validates the experience for them, making it more tangible. They are not sure they performed a task correctly because they do not have much for comparison. They need and value our assessment of their efforts at a subconscious level.. If we communicate that we think the task was done well, they will believe it also. If we do not communicate our assessment of the situation, they are left wondering. If they did not succeed at a new task, we can still validate their efforts which allows them to feel good about the risk taken and gives them permission to try again. Criticizing the child may result in his reluctance to risk further attempts. When a child receives repeated criticism for not performing up to par (and that may be very narrowly defined by certain parents), lessons are being stored in their mental computer that may very well transfer to other areas. Trying new experiences is very scary—particularly for those who have never experienced surviving failure without feeling ashamed. The lesson manifests itself in subconscious thought processes such as: *I'll keep flipping burgers at McDonald's because it's safe and I know how to do it. I'm not sure I could learn to be a _____. I won't strive for good grades because what if I really try and find out I can't cut it?*

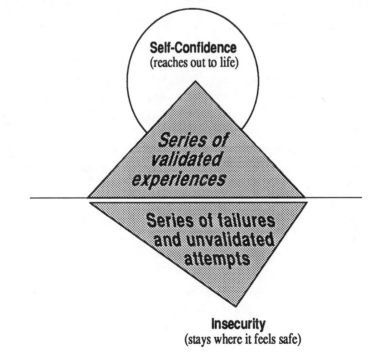

**Self-Confidence**
(reaches out to life)

*Series of validated experiences*

*Series of failures and unvalidated attempts*

**Insecurity**
(stays where it feels safe)

105

•Independent Thinking•

Developing a sense of independent thinking is also a part of self-confidence. It is important for children to learn this skill if they are to survive in our society. Independent thinking, if not taken to extreme, is respected in social and professional circles. It supplies a survival skill that will serve them well in a wide variety of situations. We can encourage our children to think independently by asking them what they think about certain situations. After they have had a moment to explore their own thought process, we can share our opinion. Here are some examples:

"Mom, does this look all right?"
"What do you think?" (A sincere question, not a sarcastic statement).

"Dad, what do you think of the draft?"
"Why do you ask? What are your thoughts?"

As the child grows and formulates opinions (sometimes strong ones), the parent has the responsibility to allow differences. It would be futile to teach independent thinking and expect the child, particularly during the teenage years, to see everything through the parent's eyes. Allowing independent thinking will be particularly challenging if the parent is a Perfectionist or Controller. A child who looks, acts, and speaks in variance to the parent's standards can be threatening. If the parent is a Rebel, a difference of opinion on the part of the child may be interpreted as "challenging him." These are the parent's issues which need attention. The consequence is smothering a skill that the child needs to live happily and successfully.

We will be challenged. That is another step in the child's progress from dependency to healthy autonomy. If we expect this and accept it as a normal behavior, we will be less likely to overcompensate by forcing the child back to an overly dependent position.

Self-confidence goes hand in hand with self-esteem. If children try new tasks, explore new talents, and seek new experiences, they will add new dimensions to their inner-self.

## Responsibility

Teaching our children to become responsible individuals provides them with a tool necessary to reach their goals in life. We wouldn't expect them to wash the car without a sponge or rag, to dry the dishes without a towel, or to mow the lawn without a lawn mower. Without a sense of responsibility regarding the work involved in reaching goals, it is very difficult to succeed at almost any endeavor. We want our children to develop an intrinsic motivation to meet meaningful challenges and to experience the pride and satisfaction involved in the completion of a task.

The development of this trait is intertwined with self-confidence and self-esteem. If we value ourselves, we will set healthy, constructive goals. If we have faith in our abilities, we will go after our goals. And if we feel a sense of responsibility, we will stay with our objectives even when the job gets tedious.

A sense of responsibility manifests itself in many forms during our children's development. It results in the completion of chores with minimal nagging, taking responsibility for one's actions, adhering to long-range goals like education and career choices, fulfilling commitments, and in leadership skills. A responsible individual is valued in every setting in our society. He or she is the one who sees what needs to be done—and does it.

Carol Koffinke

## •Consequences•

How do we go about developing a sense of responsibility in our children?  One way is to insure they experience consequences for irresponsibility.  Here is a personal example which most parents have experienced in some form or another.

When my son was eight years old, he forgot to bring a homework paper home.  The rule in his classroom (I loved it) was missed homework resulted in missed recess during which time the child would complete the assignment.  My son asked me if I could write a note that maybe I had thrown it out or lost it for him.  He turned on all the charm he could muster and it was hard not to help him escape this minor consequence.  After all, he was such a good boy, it was just a little homework assignment, and I do not like it when he's upset with me. I was able, however, to stop myself and turn on some healthy parenting awareness.  I explained to him that he would never learn to become more organized or motivated to complete his work if I lied for him. Besides that, it was dishonest.  He looked at me long and hard and I could almost feel this tiny lesson of life sinking in.

Simple lessons involving consequences can become much more profound as the child grows.  Consistency—not rigidity—is important so that the lesson can be learned and the child sees we are serious. Inconsistency confuses the way the child is able to process the lesson and prevents it from becoming part of his mental programming.  For example, if the consequence for not completing homework or chores is no TV, then we cannot change the rule just because his favorite show is on.

When my daughter became eleven years old, she began a transformation that is very common at this stage of development: that of a very responsible youngster to a pre-teen obsessed with social interests.  Phone time started interfering with homework and house-hold responsibilities.  Daydreaming about boys, dances and dating was a major distraction.  After a couple of months of unfinished chores, an unmade bed, and the arrival of bedtime before piano practicing had been accomplished, I took action. I began nagging her which is a behavior I very much dislike. Then I started feeling angry because I was being "forced" into a response that I resent—and because I was picking up some of her chores. These feelings, unaddressed, would have had a negative impact on our relationship which had been very good up to that point. So, I started deducting 50 cents for each uncompleted chore and adding fifteen minutes to her piano practicing time (normally 20 minutes) for each day she missed. This was effective since my daughter loves money and dislikes practicing piano.

We can be flexible as opposed to rigid in these cases. There were circumstances when she legitimately ran out of time in the evening (an inordinate amount of homework, gymnastics class). In these situations I offered to give her a hand. I would do a load of laundry (her chore), or suggest that she skip piano practice for the evening. If she had time to complete her tasks, then I expected her to manage her time accordingly. There are always distractions to tasks, but the child must be given the opportunity to develop the discipline to prioritize and to organize time.

### •Time Management•

The skill of time management is another part of being responsible. It involves learning that it is better to do the work at hand than to procrastinate and run out of time. We can help our children learn this when, for example, they have a project due in a two-week period. Book reports are another area where they usually need guidance to plan the work. Even daily homework assignments provide this opportunity. If a child arrives home from school, has a snack, plays or relaxes for a short time, eats dinner, watches TV and then starts his homework fifteen minutes before bedtime, he will be rushed or won't be alert enough to do it well. Most children need a little break after school before starting their homework. However, doing homework right after dinner and before watching television is very reasonable. Then, if they have too much to do before their favorite show is on, they might even think to start it before dinner. If your child watches TV up to bedtime, it works well if showers and baths are completed before the child watches that last TV show. This teaches them to plan their activities.

Evening planning presents an opportunity to teach time management, decision making, and consequences. At dinner, why not ask your children how they plan to spend the evening? Help them plan homework, bath, scheduled functions, and favorite activities (such as a game or being read to) in the allotted time. I have helped my son with time management for several years. Now, he is at the point where I only need to ask him how he plans to organize his time. He has developed a sense of priorities and timing. Our next goal is for me to drop the question and for him to assume the full responsibility.

### Discipline

Our children need to feel secure and safe if they are to grow into autonomous, healthy individuals. We can provide this security by setting healthy limits in which they can operate.

We can help our children feel safe by clearly and consistently defining the limits so that they will be familiar with the boundaries. Parents have a responsibility to keep their children safe. We are not at all haphazard about setting limits which prevent a two-year-old from playing in the streets. Likewise, the same principle applies to establishing reasonable expectations. "It is expected that you be on time for dinner and that you go to bed at _____." If we consistently (not rigidly) enforce these limits, the child learns what is expected and will most likely comply. It is important that the expectations be reasonable. This requires taking into a account the needs of the child. To do this well, we must put to use our ability to step out of "black and white" thinking and operate in the "gray" area. Perhaps our young son or daughter naturally gets drowsy around 7:00 or 8:00 PM. We should accommodate his need for sleep by creating an appropriate bedtime. On the other hand, we may have a child who needs less sleep than the average child. It would be frustrating and impossible to force that child to sleep when he is not tired. However, the parents may have a need for some private time before they go to bed. It would be reasonable to require this child to make 9:00-10:00 quiet time which would mean a quiet activity or reading for that hour (once he is old enough to read or to play independently).

Defining acceptable and unacceptable behavior is part of our job as a parent. We need to set limits for what is and is not appropriate. It is not OK for my children to be disrespectful (yell, curse, be sarcastic) to us but it is OK for them to disagree, question, or express their feelings. "I hate walking the dog! I wish we'd never gotten him!" Or, "I think that's unfair because everyone else is _____," are examples of honestly expressed feelings within the limits my husband and I have defined as acceptable. As children get older they will attempt to push the limits. In these cases I give a warning, "I don't like that tone of voice. If you want me to listen, you need to change it."

This teaching is most effective when it takes place during a child's early years, guiding the child to operate within the boundaries. Limits can be instituted at any age as long as the parent is committed to them and is willing to work with the child as he adjusts. As parents we must be able to define what is and is not acceptable for ourselves first.

My daughter went through a stage at the age of two (surprise). She would fling herself on the floor and have a tantrum when she did not get her way. I would pick her off the floor at arm's length (not holding her close which could be misconstrued as positive reinforcement), and take her to her room. Then I would tell her that she could come out whenever she stopped screaming. This was very effective with both of my children and I never had to set a particular length of time before they could leave the bedroom.  On the rare occasion when they came out too soon and continued the behavior, I repeated the procedure. Usually they came out pouting which was fine.  I did not expect them to be ecstatic for not getting their way.  But I did expect them to deal with the disappointment more appropriately.  Sometimes I took the opportunity to hug them and validate their feelings of disappointment.

Dealing with small children in such a way also gives them an opportunity to make the decision about when they are ready to come out of the room.  This is a powerful choice for a two-year-old.  *Should I stay here and scream as much as I want to, or go out and be with Mom?* This decision-making experience encourages them to start making the kind of choices that best meet their needs.  The child may need to scream for a few minutes to deal with his frustration.  But if it is done privately, this screaming does not infringe on anyone else's rights.  As the child matures, the child can use the time in his room to think about what has transpired.  I usually make that request and after awhile, go in and allow them to share with me their thoughts and feelings, then I share mine.  Sometimes, however, things are just too hot for calm discussion.

Time-outs can be important for parents too.  Sometimes *we* need to pause or we are likely to act inappropriately or back ourselves into a corner.  A dear friend had reached her limit in dealing with her children's fights over the Nintendo Video System they had purchased. She became very angry one day, grabbed the controls and said, "This will solve the problem!"  Then she threw the controls into the trash. Either she loses credibility by taking them out of the trash later, or she permanently incapacitates a system in which they had invested a good deal of money. We all feel this kind of frustration at times.  But it would be better if we could manage a time-out to think of the most effective approach.

Threats to break someone's neck, throwing out all of the toys, leaving the family, or killing someone reveal their lack of intent and become meaningless.  Children learn to tune out meaningless statements. And yet we wonder why they don't listen or respond while we attempt to threaten our way into control.

Successful discipline sometimes involves getting the child's attention. My son is virtually incapable of listening to me while the television is on. Instead of becoming frustrated with the competition, I just turn off the television while I am giving instructions. If he is not moving fast enough while getting ready for school in front the TV, a simple flick of the switch instantly increases the pace and results in less negative confrontation. Some mornings I have gotten angry with him. This starts both of our days off in an unpleasant manner.

## The Gifts

We have reviewed in some detail four priceless gifts: Self-Esteem, Self- Confidence, Responsibility, and Discipline. Look at the identified parenting traps to see how they may prevent you from giving these gifts. Now we will continue to focus on our children and how we can better connect with them.

Chapter Eight

# YOUR CHILDREN: CONNECTING WITH THEM

This chapter explores how to better understand our children and connect with them on an individual basis. We will look at how to communicate, respect their boundaries, and create quality time. Then we will learn how to respond to their unique needs and personalities in supportive and fulfilling ways.

## Communication

The quality of any relationship depends significantly on its level of communication. Since we cannot get inside someone else's thoughts and feelings, the only way we can come to understand them and be understood is by some form of communication. We transmit messages through our body language, our eyes, our touch, and our words. We can learn to receive messages through our eyes, ears, and touch.

Eye contact can positively affect our attempts to communicate with our children. When they are speaking, it is important to give them our attention. If we look at them while they speak, they know they have our attention. This is particularly important if they are communicating something of significance. On those occasions we need to put down the paper, dishes, sewing, turn off the TV or computer, and focus on our child. Eye-to-eye contact can be scary if we are not used to it, but it can help two people feel connected in a way words never can.

Touch can be a powerful tool of communication as well. Some of us may have difficulty accepting or giving any kind of affection. The pay-off in terms of nurturing and connecting to our children, however, is well worth the risk. We express a part of our love and understanding with touch. Touch is a basic need for mammals.

I am reminded of the famous experiment with the Rhesus monkey who was separated from its mother at birth and placed in a cage with a wire facsimile of a monkey. It was fed and watered but received no touch at all. The monkey died. Human beings usually find some way to survive even if there was little affection from parents or caregivers. But our children deserve our loving touch. If deprived, they too will inherit the family legacy of finding another way to survive. A hug, a pat on the shoulder, scratching the back, a ruffling of the hair, and holding hands are a few ways in which we can communicate on this level with our children.

Listening is a much ignored aspect of communication. But it comprises 50% of the communication process. As we learn to become more verbally proficient, we can also learn to become better listeners. Hear what your children are really saying. They need to know that their ideas, thoughts, feelings and problems are important to you—that *they* are important. Children seem to have a special radar that detects when we are not listening to them. The result is some sense of being rejected. That doesn't mean that we must drop everything anytime our child opens his mouth. Remember the happy medium? There are times when we need to have uninterrupted time with ourselves or others. But it is important that we get back to the child about whatever it was he was trying to tell us.

Communicating feelings to our children will help them feel more connected to us. This can be done in a way that is appropriate for their particular age. If the child's behavior has upset us, we need to tell him about it. If we are experiencing some problems not relating to the child, we should communicate that as well without going into detail. We might say we are dealing with a work problem, but that it has nothing to do with them. This frees them from trying to figure out what they did "wrong." We also need to share our ideas about life, God, politics, people, and work. As we open our minds and hearts to them, our children get to know who we are as people and they feel more connected. This connection is necessary so they won't feel alone in the world.

Communication is a two-way street. Listening is more involved than just hearing the words. Regardless of how trivial a problem seems to us, it may be very important to our children. Try to remember what it was like to be eight or ten or twelve. Our children need to feel what they say is important. Sometimes it helps to share how we survived a similar situation. We can't fix the majority of their problems. But allowing them to talk the crisis out will make it seem much less powerful and more manageable. When children feel alone, their problems can seem monumental. Peers and chemicals become powerful means of support or escape, for children feel they have no safe place to turn.

## Boundaries

In Chapter Six, we explored the concept of setting healthy boundaries from the parent's point of view. There is another perspective that is important in our relationship with our children: teaching children to set healthy boundaries. As parents, we need to examine our children's requirement for established boundaries. If we respect this need and act in a way that encourages the development of a clearly defined set of boundaries, we help our child formulate an identity. As we discussed in the section on discipline, children who have had limits set by their parents will feel the most secure. Now we have a responsibility to teach them how to set their own limits. This is crucial for identity formation.

| No boundaries, no sense of self | Some boundaries, developing identity | A whole person with boundaries |

How do we encourage our children to establish boundaries? Here are a few ideas:

- Respecting their need for privacy (closing the bathroom door, changing clothes, phone calls, diaries).
- Allowing them their own space.
- Respecting their need to not be touched or hugged at a particular time.
- Respecting their need to be alone.

This kind of respect on our part gives our children permission to set and assert personal boundaries that are necessary if they are to develop the "self" that many children from dysfunctional families struggle to develop. The lack of a "self" prevents the personality from maturing and evolving. The immature nature of the individual becomes part of the "Injured Child" that is unable to grow. We must allow our children to develop this self concept by experimenting with who they are and identifying their needs. When we show their developing self *respect*, it nurtures a sense of *self-respect*.

We should also teach our children to set limits with others. Here are some examples:

- Addressing a situation where they are being treated poorly by their peers.
- Validating their position when they are treated poorly by an adult (such as a teacher or neighbor).
- Supporting them when they take risks to assert their needs with others appropriately.

Teaching our children to set limits helps them sort through the confusion of their rights and needs versus the rights and needs of others. If we are skilled at teaching, our children will also learn to think beyond the "black and white" and into the "gray." No one is always right and no one comes first all of the time.

The children learn that Mom and Dad respect their needs and therefore they must have a right to them. They can learn, within reason, that they deserve to have others respect those needs. This lesson can permeate their self-esteem, their self-confidence, and the nature of other relationships.

## Quality Time

With so many families today consisting of two working parents, or a single working parent, the cliche "quality time" becomes an essential part of healthy parenting. As a working mother I often put myself on a guilt trip as the old tapes of "Good Moms stay home and raise their children" played over and over in my head. I vacillated between staying home with children and working. Most working mothers struggle with one of two conflicts:

1. I need outside stimulation but I want to be the best parent I can be.
2. We need the money but I want to be the best parent I can be.

Is it possible to work and be a good parent or must it be an either/ or situation? My own personal need to work was strong enough to result in resentment if I forced myself to remain at home. That resentment interfered with my attitude and ability to parent the way I wanted to.

We can be great parents and still work outside the home if we use well the little time we have with our children. If we work, we need to make our children a priority for a period to time in those non-working hours. How we do this depends on our schedule and the number of children. One way is to insure some one-on-one time with each child. That may not be possible every day but should be possible once a week. This is a time for you and your child to be together and connect by either a shared activity or talking.

My daughter and I seldom had trouble finding one-on-one time together because we have always shared a number of interests such as cooking, shopping, and music. These kinds of activities can be easily modified to include a child at any age. My son and I, however, seemed to have very little one-on-one time except when I would make him sit down and listen as I read him a book. Mutual activities seemed to be much more natural with my husband and son, but my husband spent little time with our daughter. We were unhappy about the few opportunities we had with our opposite-sexed child, so we decided to create some of these opportunities ourselves. My husband began driving our daughter to and from piano lessons on Saturday mornings. This was about a fifteen minute drive and gave him time to talk to her about school, music, and friends. I started taking my son with me on short errands. We would talk about school, friends, and sports.

For a number of years I dropped everything at 8:00 PM and made my children a snack. Then I would sit with them while they watched a favorite TV show. I tried to do this regularly even though I really despised some of these evening programs. This seemed to be a high point of their evening. Homework, practice and baths were out of the way and it was time to relax. They were glad that I made their quiet time a priority in my evening.

Children also appreciate it when parents take time to play games with them. This is an activity which can be mutually enjoyed—especially when the children get old enough to move on from *"Candyland"* and the card game *"War."* Family games can be great fun as long as Mom and Dad are able to relax and do not become too impatient with the children's pace.

## Boys Versus Girls

Till now, we have looked at our children in general terms. But to gain a deeper understanding of them, we need to consider their individuality. The example regarding my children's interests in music and sports shows that there are differences in the sexes. But that does not mean that activities need to be sexually specific.

For some reason, my daughter was always interested in tradition-ally "feminine" activities, and my son in traditionally "masculine" activities. As parents we make a big mistake by having such traditional expectations and projecting them upon our children. I prefer to consider these activities "gentle" as opposed to "feminine," and "active" as opposed to "masculine". Nurturing a gentle and active/assertive side in both sexes will help our children adapt to the many challenges encountered throughout life. Girls who are not assertive will end up with issues similar to the People-Pleaser (see Chapter Four) and will have difficulty taking care of their needs. Boys who are not gentle will expend a great deal of time and energy convincing others that they are tough. This "gentle" side is as much a part of being human as is the need to love and be loved. A boy's gentle side will help him relate to others and express love. We need to help our children develop their natural interests and encourage them accordingly. To do this, parents must resolve possible stereotypes.

Consider these questions:

- Are you comfortable with your daughter playing sports?
- Are you comfortable with your son's interest in the Arts? Cooking?
- Do you allow your daughter to express anger appropriately?
- Do you allow your son to cry?

Affirmative answers indicate that you are avoiding stereotypes.

The most difficult stereotype for parents to break is "Boys don't cry." Fathers fear their sons may grow up to be "sissies." Some mothers fear that their son will grow up to be a "mama's boy."

Being a therapist and a mother, I really thought that I knew how to handle this crying issue. I encouraged my son to cry whenever he needed to, validating that this was OK as the tears flowed. It soon became apparent that there was one issue my husband and I failed to discuss before marriage: how to raise sons. We each had strong opinions about how crying should be handled with the male child— opposite opinions.

I remember distinctly the day our eight-year-old son came home crying because another child had pushed him down (and hard, too). My husband started chastising him for crying. I became so infuriated with my husband that I could hardly contain myself. Through clenched teeth, I requested to speak with him in the bedroom. Behind closed doors, I released my rage. How dare he not let this child cry because he was hurt? What was he trying to teach him anyway? To be a machine? To be able to cut off feelings that were real? To *repress feelings?* To a therapist/mother, this is comparable to someone pulling out your child's fingernails in front of you.

My husband began to explain that boys need to hide tears in some situations for their own protection. He said that if a boy is pushed by another boy and falls to the ground crying, he is likely to be kicked and beaten up pretty badly. This made some sense to me. I shared with him my fears that if he is forced to hide his feelings behind a wall of toughness, he would have difficulty later on in his relationships. I tried to make him understand that feelings are what connect human beings and that I desperately wanted our son to know who he is on an emotional level.

We were both operating from fears that had been uncommunicated until this incident. His fear was not so much that his son would grow up to be a "sissy." He feared that our son could get hurt often and badly if he did not toughen up in certain areas. I feared that our son would lose touch with his feelings after hiding them over a period of time. There was some merit and some exaggeration to both sides. However, through discussion, we each began to appreciate the other's perspective. Again, a happy medium is the answer. Not black. Not white. Gray.

## Birth Order

There has been a myth floating around for about one zillion years that to be a good parent you should treat all your children the same. This was the best way to be "fair" and many parents take this erroneous advice very seriously. Accordingly, many make a point to measure and divide their material goods, as well as their love, among their children. This attitude is as rigid as many of the other attitudes that we have examined in this book.

My great grandmother used to bake bread. If she did not have enough loaves to give to all of us, she would not give away any. "I don't have enough for your sisters, and I don't want to hurt anyone's feelings." I also clearly remember her counting out cookies so that no one was given less than someone else. Her motive was beautiful—she wanted us to feel equally loved. Unfortunately, love is a hard thing to slice evenly. It can be real exhausting to try, too.

Sharon Wegscheider-Cruse states in her film *The Family Trap*, "If everyone's the same, then no one is special." Much to the credit of the ACOA movement, and the contributions of Cruse, Claudia Black and Janet Woititz, we have been given the opportunity to see that children develop differently and actually may differ in what they need from us. The birth order itself can have a powerful impact on a child's personality. We can best support our children's healthy development by becoming aware of their different needs.

Let us examine birth order and how it relates to the four classic roles identified by Sharon Wegscheider-Cruse and described in Chapter Three. In that chapter, you focused on yourself as a child. Now identify certain behavioral characteristics within your own children. This process will be helpful in understanding what each of your children needs from you.

But how will fitting your children into stereotypes help you address their unique needs? Each of your children is different. Studying your children individually will provide a deeper understanding of who they are as people. Then you can modify what you learn to fit your own situation. The roles are just a starting point. You may find that your child is a blend of roles, or switches from one role to another. Responding flexibly to your children will help guide them properly down the appropriate path at the appropriate time.

## First-Born

These children may have many of the characteristics of the Hero (Chapter Three). They are overachievers who tend to be very mature for their age. They usually have a strong need to be liked and may exhibit people-pleasing kinds of behaviors. They are probably engaged in school activities, are good students, popular, and responsible around the house. It is possible that a younger sibling may fall into this role, but it is far less common. It is always best, however, to keep an open mind.

What could these children need from us? They sound perfect, don't they? The challenge lies in the fact that their identity becomes more and more attached to their accomplishments as they receive praise for their performance (good grades, friends, elected offices). They are what they do. This attachment is dangerous because it encourages them to deny their humanness—something they must come to terms with if they are to lead healthy lives. We are all human. That means imperfect. These children could spend their lives trying to convince themselves otherwise. What a waste! We need to encourage them to be gentle with themselves and validate their right to make mistakes—and not be perfect. It helps if we are able to model this ourselves. If they bring home a "B" instead of the usual "A," we must be careful not to act like it is the end of the world. We need to encourage them to have fun and be children. If we feed their desire to be an adult, they will most likely respond and an entire childhood could be missed. By skipping this stage, they will suffer later in life. Healthy development is a step-by-step process—not a gargantuan leap forward from infancy into adulthood.

Remember the game, "Mother, May I?" The child playing Mother would lead the rest of the children to where she was by telling them to take so many baby or giant steps forward. Each child had to ask the question, "Mother, May I?" before he was given permission to move. The Hero, in his people pleasing way, asks for permission to skip childhood—to take giant steps forward toward adulthood. Playing the Mother, we are apt to say, "Yes, you may," because they are doing so well in all of their endeavors. We may find ourselves feeding into their desire to be an instant adult, perfectly mature, because there is a payoff for us. It feels good to have the teachers rave and the neighbors turn green. It can also take a load off of us to have a child who assumes household responsibilities. These behaviors are desirable to a certain extent. But we do not want our Hero to be so attached to success that a disappointment such as not getting voted president of the class becomes unbearable. We don't want him so tied into being perfect that he beats up on himself mercilessly if he forgets to do a chore. More than anything, this child needs permission from us to be human.

### Younger Child/Scapegoat

If you recall, the Scapegoat refers to the children who are the rebels—the defiant ones. They are the children who need to be different and seek negative attention because they are afraid to compete with the Hero. They think this is the only way they can establish their "place" in the family. Often, the Scapegoat will be the second or a middle child. His or her behavior is usually a reaction to the family's treatment of the Hero, or a reaction to some family stress.

We can minimize the child's reaction to being the "younger" sibling by not comparing the children. If these children sense that our self-esteem is very locked into how they behave and perform, they will use their behavior and performance to gain power over us. We must prevent our identity from becoming enmeshed in the child's, and our self-esteem from becoming so dependent on outside influences.

Also, you may need to take a look at the marriage. John Bradshaw, author of *The Family*, determined that many children who get into trouble are acting out the troubled relationship between the parents. The parents ignore their own pain and obsess over the "bad" kid.

We also need to raise our parenting awareness. Remember, hurt and/or fear are often emotions underneath the defiance. When this child acts out, we can attempt to help him understand what it was that hurt or frightened him. These matters will usually not be simple like falling off of a bicycle or the Boogeyman. They will be intangible hurts such as rejection, and fear that we don't love him. This child needs to be encouraged to become aware of and comfortable with his real feelings so that they are expressed appropriately and so that he can feel loved for who he is.

## Middle Child/Lost Child

This is the quiet one, the child who avoids conflict and does not assert his rights, the one we don't have to worry about because the last thing they want is attention. He may be the middle child, the youngest, or the oldest.

When these children become upset and go to their room, it is tempting for the parent to let them go. That's because these children react in quiet and non-demanding ways. These children, however, will not learn how to connect with other human beings in fulfilling ways unless we intervene. They live a lonely life as children and adults. Avoiding people may become comfortable and relating to others might become frightening.

When these children become upset, we need to ask them how they are feeling about what happened. If they don't know, we need to help them find out by sharing a situation from our past or by describing how we would possibly feel if we were them. If they retreat because an older sibling has overpowered them and they have relinquished their rights, we might try to help them understand that they are as important as anyone else in the family. "How does it feel to always give in to your sister?" "Why do you always give in to your brother?" These children may need support if they are to take a risk and assert themselves. We can help by talking to the older siblings about this family issue, and by encouraging them to accept the Lost Child's feelings and needs.

These children need to be given emotional attention in other ways as well. If they are avoiding conflict and won't express feelings, they have already started the process of disconnecting from their emotional selves. The sooner we become aware of this child's emotional needs, the better.

When my son was seven, he occasionally wet the bed. The therapist/mother in me was careful not to make a big deal about it or to add to his escalating sense of shame. However, one morning I was running late for work. When I went in to wake him up for school, I discovered everything in the bed was wet: sheets, pillows, and comforter. I was not particularly gentle as I stripped off the bedclothes. Then I caught a glimpse of this small child sitting naked on the floor, shoulders bent over, head hung down, knees pulled up to his chest, arms wrapped around his knees. He looked so small and fragile and hurt. I stopped myself and sat down on the only dry corner of the bed.

"Is there anything that is upsetting you or that maybe you feel afraid of?" I said.

He hesitated for a moment and then barely lifted his face. "Well", he said in a small voice, "there is something I am kind of afraid of."

"What," I asked preparing myself to interpret in psychological terms some deeply hidden fear.

"I'm scared to get up in the dark to go to the bathroom," he said.

That day, I got a night light—and that was the end of the crisis. Don't I wish they were all that simple. More importantly, I learned my son was unable to tell me about his fear. I had to ask him and encourage him to express the fear.

## Youngest Child/Mascot

This is the cute one, the clown, the baby. He is the one we won't discipline when his behavior is not quite up to par.

To respond appropriately to the needs of this child, we must become aware of our own desire to keep him dependent on us. It is tough to let go of our children as they grow and become more and more independent—particularly the youngest. It means giving up certain parental functions for the last time.

I couldn't wait for the day my first child could tie her own shoes and dress herself. Yet I found myself still tying my second (last) child's shoes when he was eight years old. These youngest children not only have Mom and Dad who are reluctant to relinquish certain functions, but also other siblings who are willing to help this child with whatever Mom or Dad doesn't. Unfortunately, these children can grow up and get married without having learned to butter their own bread. This child needs us to encourage his independence and sense of responsibility no matter how cute he is. He needs us to set consequences for irresponsible behavior and to not falter regardless of how deep the dimples. Requiring a serious attitude at serious times and preventing siblings from protecting him are also part of responding to this child's needs. Otherwise, we encourage his dependence, irresponsibility, and immaturity. Because we love this child, we must prepare him to fend for himself when he gets older.

Let me share another family experience. This one showed me the differences between my two children and how each needed something different from me. My daughter, being the oldest, has definite Hero tendencies. My son (two years younger) is a combination Lost Child/ Mascot. It was the end of the 1986 school year. We had just moved to a new area. The new school system had a more advanced curriculum and both children experienced a slight academic set-back. Due to my son's age (born in November), maturity level, and struggle to keep up in the new school, the teacher and I decided that it would be best if he repeated the first grade.

After the last day of school, the children walked in the house with their report cards. My daughter stormed in first, looking like she was ready to start World War III. She scrunched her report card in a ball, threw it in the corner, and stomped upstairs. I picked up the card, smoothed it out, and beheld three A's and four B's. Next, my son meandered in with a big smile on his face and handed me his report card. "What do these D's mean anyway, Mom," he asked as he calmly walked to the TV and turned it on.

Four years later I still have to be firm with my son about homework. And I still console my daughter when she does not do well. But each of them is changing. My daughter is able to accept the fact that she can't be perfect *all* of the time, and my son has even decided on his own to rewrite a few assignments because they weren't neat enough. If I had treated them the same, either my daughter would be neurotic or my son would still be in first grade. My daughter does *not* need to be urged to perform better. My son does *not* need to be encouraged to relax his expectations.

Remember, our children are special. Each needs us in a unique way and will develop a sense of his own specialness as we connect and respond to him as an individual.

### Your Adult Children

If your children are grown, you may wonder what possible influence you can have over changing the quality and nature of your relationship with them. Opportunities to teach and guide them may have been minimal for years. Remember, modeling is the most powerful teaching tool you possess. It is never too late to affect the relationship by modeling the changes yourself. If you want more contact, initiate it. If you want less contact, establish some limits. If you want less fighting, stop participating. If you want more affection, touch them more.

Be patient. Old lessons die hard. The effort will be well worth it.

## Grown Children: Forgiving Yourself

I was anxious when my parents read this book. I was unsure of their reaction. The feedback was good although the journey was painful for them. We talked about what this book would mean to Adult Children whose own children are grown and are estranged. A feeling of helplessness is inevitable as one gains insight into the past but is unable to change it.

Although my mother has excellent relationships with all of us, she still feels guilty over certain aspects of her parent role. She knows she couldn't have been too bad a mother or we wouldn't love her like we do. Still, regrets are there.

I realized then that most of us think we could have done a better job raising our kids. We are looking at the past with wiser eyes and perceptions. The person who responded to the many challenges of raising children did so with much less experience than the same person who looks back at those years and judges. Remember this and be gentle with yourself.

Our mind often leads us to the past regardless of our willingness to go along. This book has led you on a scheduled, calculated journey into the past for the purpose of learning and healing. We have the choice to learn, make the necessary changes, validate ourselves for doing the best we could, and let it go. The other choice is an exercise in self-flagellation. This is often the result of an unscheduled journey where our heart plays victim to our mind's need to review, review, review.

## I *Did* Do That To My Kids

I particularly want to address those readers whose children are grown and estranged. This is usually a painful situation for both parties. If you are a parent, there are regrets with which to deal: regrets

131

that you were not the parent you wished you had been; regrets that you did not get what you needed from your parents; regrets that you didn't know more than you knew. A feeling of loss is created because our regrets are tied to the past. Now that time is gone. Grieve these losses as you would any loss. The pain is worthy of tears. Consider counseling if you are unable to cry or if the losses seem overwhelming.

I offer this poem as an expression of these regrets. If it will help open a door with your children, perhaps you can share it with them.

### Regrets

When you look at me, my distant child,
I wonder who it is you see.
The one who often let you down,
Who never seemed to turn around?
The one who wouldn't come too close,
Withholding what you needed most?

When peering in the looking glass
With eyes that fear to face the past,
I often see the same outcast.
The one who seemed to put you last,
Whose finger pointed you to blame,
And bestowed a legacy of shame.

But know that when I hurt inside,
This aging body cannot hide
The secret me I feel exposed,
A child behind a door thought closed.
A little child who did not grow,
A hand-me-down from long ago.

I was a child, hard to believe
Who watched for Santa on Christmas Eve,
Who needed a song, a smile, a touch,
Who wanted to be loved so much.
Who hid from the dark, cried when she fell,
Whose hopes and dreams she longed to tell.

A child whose cries were seldom heard,
Whose hopes and dreams were smothered tight,
Whose song was silenced with a word,
Who tucked herself in bed at night,
Whose laughter trickled to a sigh,
Whose fear could leave her paralyzed.

A child whose feet and dress size grew,
Who looked mature, but no one knew
She was really nothing but a fraud,
Still a child, trapped and walled.
Trying hard to play the part,
And hide the child lost in the dark.

When you were born she swore on high
You'd never, ever have to cry.
Your fears she'd gently kiss away.
She'd sing a song to you each day.
She'd tuck you into bed each night.
You were her chance to do it right.

Look again, my child, and see
The child who hurts inside of me.
Who loved you with her heart and soul,
But didn't know, just didn't know
How to give that love to you.
I wanted to.  I wanted to.

What will make the difference now is what you do with your feelings. If you're feeling like you made a lot of mistakes, you can go on a major guilt trip or take the initiative and share what you have learned about yourself with your children. Chances are, they will be receptive to what you have to say. If not, allow them the space to hurt some more, knowing you gave it a try. In a couple of months, approach them again. You are not responsible for how your grown children respond to what you have to say. You are no longer in a position to put on the bandage. They have choices—to open the door to healing or keep it closed. In time, they may open the door slightly to get a better look at you. When they feel safe, they will open it.

My mother found out about her father's death through the newspaper. "Mom," I asked her one day, "if your father had called you on the phone and said something like, 'I've been learning about myself and my relationship with you. Could I come over and speak with you about it?' How would you have responded?"

Without hesitation, she replied, "I would have been the happiest person in the world."

I believe this would be the response of most estranged children.

**References**
Bradshaw, John. *It's Not My Problem.* A film.
Wegscheider-Cruse, Sharon. (1976). *Family Trap.* A film. Rapid City, SD. Onsite Training and Consulting.
Wegscheider-Cruse, Sharon. (1981) *Another Chance.* Palo Alto, CA. Science and Behaviors Books, Inc.

Chapter Nine

# YOUR PARENTS

Examining our present relationships with our parents is the final step which completes the rite into full adulthood. Unless we can look at this relationship honestly, accepting it for its strengths and weaknesses, we may be discouraged from developing a healthy sense of autonomy. If we are untreated Adult Children, that relationship can maintain power over us (see Enmeshment in Chapter Four).

Let's explore the importance of establishing an adult to adult relationship with our parents beyond what is traditionally considered the "dependent years". There is a period of time when we are dependent physically and emotionally on our parents. But at some point we need to grow out of that. Let's also examine our need to move toward forgiveness.

## Growing Up

If our Injured Child has not had an opportunity to heal, we may find ourselves being stuck in the role of child as we relate to our parents. Evidence of this obstacle can be seen in behaviors such as still needing their approval for our actions and/or decisions, and by still allowing them to push old "buttons" to manipulate us. We may still find difficulty in asserting our own needs with them. Or we may still find ourselves assessing life through the filter called Mom and Dad.

Even when we have made progress in our recovery, we may find that our relationship with our parents presents the biggest challenge when we implement changes. So we see the People-Pleaser compromising himself in this relationship, the Rebel acting out, and the Entertainer joking despite their success in changing these behaviors in other areas of their lives. We may find that our parents can still hurt us deeper than anyone, and enrage us beyond belief. Hypervigilance, a familiar childhood companion, may raise its nasty head when we are around Mom and/or Dad. How can we be so intimidated when we have spent a number of years working through these issues? As we walk in that old house, sometimes it seems as if everything we think we've built in recovery falls through a trap door.

Don't feel alone if you are experiencing some (or all) of these feelings. The family of origin is the "slipperiest" area for most of us when it comes to exhibiting changed behavior and expressing emotional growth.

Why is that, you ask? Diaz and O'Gorman have discovered in their work with young COA's (Children of Alcoholics) that the sense of loyalty to parents is unbelievably strong in dysfunctional families. One reason for this is that the child's inner-self is somehow injured, hampering growth and fostering dependency. As any injured animal becomes dependent while healing, an individual will find it difficult to become independent and establish a healthy sense of autonomy in a similar situation (see Chapter Four, *You The Adult, Injured Child*). COA's, even after their bodies grow into adults, will experience an emotional connection to their parents which can continue to hold a magnetic power over them. Many try to break this hold by moving away, thinking the further the distance, the less the hold. This effort does not solve the problem. The old issues that these Adult Children had hoped to leave behind pop up like gremlins everywhere they turn.

I have seen these dynamics played out over and over again with the Adult Children. The "tie that binds" can sometimes be a shackle where no one seems to have the key. We need to develop a less enmeshed relationship with our parents. To unlock the shackle allows the tie to become more like an elastic thread that can allow us to move freely and grow—a thread we can even cut if necessary.

Most children will eventually assert their need for emotional autonomy. As I look at my own family, I see the traumatic break coming earlier, directly proportional to our birth order. For my youngest sister, the time came at age fourteen when she ran away from home for the first time. For my next sister, the break started at age seventeen when she refused to listen to my parents and dated a man addicted to heroin. For my next sister, the first real crisis came at age eighteen when she went away to college and partied instead of studying, quitting after the first year. My next sister was twenty years old when she quit college and married a boy my parents wouldn't even allow in the yard.

Being the oldest, I was the late bloomer. When I was twenty-nine I realized that I was in a marriage that wasn't going to work. The conflict of deciding what to do drove me into therapy as I developed a case of insomnia, and could not sleep well for months. Choosing divorce meant disappointing my parents, probably for the first time in my life. It also meant rejecting the mental programming that said marriage is forever and "good" Moms don't divorce their child's father. To stay in the marriage would have meant compromising my basic need for a loving, intimate relationship—or seeking this kind of relationship outside the marriage. The day that I poured myself a glass of wine to chase the ever elusive nap, (preceded by a night when I drank Nyquil to shut down my mind,) was the day I knew I needed help. I immediately sought counseling and eventually resolved the conflict.

A relationship between parent and adult child is the healthiest when its nature is adult to adult, not parent to child. When we are able to maintain our adult identity even in the presence of our parents, we have dealt effectively with issues of dependency and enmeshment. This does not mean that we cannot be comforted by our parents if they are available to us and we are experiencing discomfort or pain. Nor does it mean that we cannot comfort them when they may need us. Remember, we don't deal in blacks and whites anymore. Gray is OK.

If one is to gain autonomy, the pathological attachment to parents must be broken. This involves coming to terms with realities in the family. This can be particularly difficult since it may involve the destruction of some myth that probably helped the individual survive while growing up. We discussed denial much earlier in the book. Yes, denial prevents a family from dealing effectively with a crisis. But it can also be a means of survival. Therapy is often helpful in the letting go of certain illusions regarding our family of origin.

Recovery can be a difficult time. There is a strong tendency to maintain the attachment and a strong pull to be part of the family on their terms. At the same time there is a fear of being "sucked" into the ongoing dysfunction. This can be tempting because it is safe, familiar and somewhat predictable. Risking new ways of interacting is like walking down a very crooked path in a very dark forest. We don't know what will jump out at each turn and we feel a gnawing sense of anxiety with each step.

If we are to connect with our parents in adulthood, they may need to do some work as well. Our own recovery can act as a catalyst, although our parent's recovery is not something we have any control over. Until they are able to make needed changes, we must find some safe way to connect with our parents while setting the necessary boundaries. Stephanie Brown refers to this as "pockets of entry." Examples of setting limits are: "I will not remain in a conversation with you when you insist on criticizing my husband," or, "You cannot drink in my house."

How much time and work it takes to set boundaries with our parents varies from individual to individual. If asserting your needs—even gently—leaves you feeling scared to death, you may benefit from outside help. Your intentions are to act like an adult with your parents, yet the behavior does not seem to follow. A chasm often exists between what we want and how we act. Sometimes we need to build a bridge if the chasm is too deep (fear of falling) or too wide (impossible to achieve). Therapy can help build that bridge.

### Forgiveness

Another step toward healthy autonomy is forgiveness. This does not necessarily mean that our parents have been ogres. For some of us there are only uncomfortable moments from the past that we seem destined to relive over and over again. These memories can create feelings of resentment as we wish things had gone differently. For others, there are major traumas that have been experienced. These need to be worked through to the point of forgiveness. Blaming, hatred, and resentment are powerful chains that can shackle us to the past and to our parents.

Sometimes, before we can get to the point of forgiveness, our Injured Child must be willing to lance the wound. Private therapy, group therapy, and intensive programs can help. Deciding to forgive may mean commitment to therapy. Forgiveness is not spontaneously achieved just because one makes the decision. Some say that they have forgiven the past when, in fact, they are seeking to escape the pain associated with it. Unfortunately, the wound still exists. When we move instantaneously from resentment to forgiveness we repress the pain. The negative feelings linger and result in either continued enmeshment (negative feelings connect as well as positive) or abandonment on our part.

If we remain in the childlike position with our parents, forgiveness will never come about. It isn't necessary. Children don't really *have* to forgive their parents. To them, in their dependent stance, the parents are powerful and all-knowing. So the dysfunctional relationship continues to send messages to the Adult Child such as: "Parents are right, children are wrong. Parents are good, children are bad."

At some point we want to see our parents as human beings who may have made a mistake or two. In the journey we have shared thus far, we have returned to this theme of human imperfection several times. We start to perceive our parents as people who have strengths and weaknesses. A small child is unable to step far enough away to ascertain this. An ability to broaden our perspective in such a way, however, indicates significant growth.

Sometimes there exists a coalition which pits one parent against the other. We may be very much aware of Mom's flaws but idolize Dad, or we may be able to take Dad's negative inventory in our sleep while Mom remains the Saint. Many of the Adult Children I have worked with have shared such opposite perceptions of their parents. "Dad was drunk, but Mom was a martyr." "Dad was never there, but Mom was everything to us." "Mom was a drunk, but Dad was kind and gentle." "Mom was a bitch, but Dad was loving and affectionate." A division of loyalty is fairly understandable when considering the fact that Mom and Dad rarely function as a team in dysfunctional families. Try to remember that no one is all good or all bad, all right or all wrong.

If you find yourself unwilling to forgive, the questions below will broaden your perception.

1) Did your parent/s come from a dysfunctional family?
2) What did you want from them—and not receive?
4) Were their feelings and individuality validated?
5) Did they learn healthy ways to express love?
6) Did they receive loving support as they experienced their own humanness?

If you don't know the answers to these questions, you should ask your parents what it was like for them when they were growing up. You may see them as children with unmet needs and unfulfilled dreams—and gain a greater understanding of them.

If feeling love for your parents seems like a remote and undesirable place to be, consider this: it is possible to experience a love for parents that is not personal but more global in nature. All of us will experience pain in our lives and this is one human condition that we all share. Love emerges from universal understanding which communicates, "I love you for all you have experienced and struggled against in your life. I love you for your efforts to survive situations which you did not ask to experience. I love you for giving me life."

We can develop the ability to forgive. We can let go of that old emotional baggage. The effort blesses both our parents and ourselves.

Chapter Ten

# YOUR FAMILY

So far, our journey has led us to an exploration of our relationships with ourselves, children and parents. It is now imperative that we take a look at the family as a whole. This way we will learn how to nurture and encourage cohesiveness. Our goal is to understand certain needs of the family as it functions together. How the family functions together and interrelates is what comprises the family system. This family system acts as a diving board from which each individual embarks to face the world. If the board is well-maintained and the dives are well-taught, they will be well-executed and beautiful to watch. If the board is maintained but the diver is not trained, the result will be less satisfying.

Likewise, if the family is working well together and has properly prepared the individual members for embarking independently upon the world, the task has been well-executed. However, if the family system is dysfunctional (like the broken board), the individual is unable to freely leave and will be tied to it because the system cannot support him on his journey.

Another way to understand how a healthy family prepares each individual for adulthood, is to think of the family as an oasis. Individuals receive what they need but at some point they must face the adventure of seeing what is beyond the visible sand dunes. So the venturing nomads fill their flasks with water first, then leave the safety of the oasis. They may find themselves returning over and over to refill their flasks until they finally arrive at their destination. They probably were not sure where they were going. But by risking the journey they were able to realize where they wanted to go and learned how to get there. Yet the oasis was always there for them.

## Creating an Oasis

How can we create this oasis and insure that the diving board is well-maintained? If you have done some of the work in the earlier portion of this book, you are well on your way. In addition, it is helpful to establish a family structure that has boundaries and characteristics which make it easily recognizable by it members. We can create a secure system like the oasis so the individuals know when they are "home" and where they can receive their sustenance.

Husbands and fathers going out to face the pressures of the job and struggling to survive the male cultural values of being strong, competitive, and under control need to have a special place where they can return. They need to have a place that will allow them to relax, be themselves, and have their humanness - not their maleness - validated. They need a place to let their defenses down without being afraid of being attacked.

Wives and mothers charging out to meet the Super Mom/goddess image expected of the modern day woman need to have a special place where they can return. They need a place to be accepted and loved for their humanness and spirit rather than performance.

Teenagers who often feel they are drowning as they test the waters of adulthood, learning most lessons the hard way, need to have a special place where they can return. They need a place where they can briefly regress to the safety of childhood. They need a place where they can be accepted and supported regardless of who they are that day—a confident adult or a skinned-up child.

Little children who slowly begin to realize that the world doesn't revolve around them and that they must start experiencing certain endeavors without Mom or Dad need to have a special place where they can recuperate from taking risks in becoming independent. They need a place where they feel their needs are important, where they know Mom and Dad are always there.

The family can be a haven for all of us. It can be a place where we know our changing needs can be met and where we are loved even if we've developed a pot belly, have a well-established set of crow's feet, been rejected by our peers, or were made to stay after school.

Let's try to remember that the members of our family will experience problems at some time or another. As Scott Peck states in the opening of his book, *The Road Less Traveled*, "Life is difficult." Truly, some problems will be more severe than others. If we can remember that experiencing difficulties is to be expected in families and resolving them as a group creates the glue that hold the family together, the difficulties will seem much less powerful. This brings us back to the restatement of a truth at the start of this book:

## There Is No Such Thing As A Perfect Family!

Experiencing problems is not an indictment of our parenting or the health of our family. An attitude of, "What can we learn from this?" and, "I welcome this opportunity to bond with my family in resolving this," will encourage growth in the inter-family relationships.

## Family Traditions

How do we further define our family character? It is important to establish some family traditions. If you came from a family where the dysfunction resulted in chaos and absence of any family unity, your growing up experiences may be void of any family traditions that can be passed to your children. In that case, it is nice to start your own traditions and get some input from other family members about what these traditions could be.

Traditions can be big or small. When I grew up, Christmas was fraught with traditions—including Santa decorating the tree, taking turns in opening gifts and Christmas Dinner. I needed to modify those traditions slightly in my family in order to incorporate my husband's family traditions with mine. There was the Sunday morning tradition of church with a family lunch afterward. Hot chocolate together with my father was a tradition for anyone upset about friends, school and dates.

Sometimes traditions change as the family changes. It was traditional in my husband's family to have baked beans and hot dogs every Saturday night. His father cooked (I liked that part). My husband, however, met with some resistance as he fought to continue this tradition in our family (our children do not care for baked beans). Some things die very hard.

Traditions can be renegotiated. As my sisters and I married and started our own families, we stopped celebrating every Christmas and Thanksgiving at Mom's. Now we spread around the holiday get-togethers. This seems to have worked out better for everyone, especially Mom.

My children love to be tucked in every night, even though they are thirteen and eleven. I don't know when that small tradition will be renegotiated—I'm trying to keep an open mind. They also like a waffle breakfast on Sundays.

Some traditions can be expensive, like a yearly vacation. Other ideas are a weekly game night, a nightly story, a Sunday brunch, or a monthly restaurant outing. Sometimes it is difficult to get a new tradition going. Talk it over with your family and keep the ideas reasonable. When you *do* decide on a new tradition, keep it very consistent so that it becomes a part of your family life.

## Family Boundaries

Families also benefit from established boundaries that may be unspoken but are clearly understood. Non-acceptance of physical or verbal abuse of another family member would seem to be a basic boundary that needs to be established. Children need to know that it is unacceptable to physically hurt each other in any way. The difference between verbal abuse and appropriately expressed feelings needs to be taught, the former not being tolerated. When our children are instructed to respect each other, the individuals within the family system feel protected and secure. In the process, they are learning the difference between healthy anger and verbal abuse.

We can also establish family boundaries by expecting rules to be respected. *Ask before you use someone else's belongings. Knock before entering someone else's room.* Besides helping children establish appropriate personal boundaries, these kinds of rules establish values in a family system that become a part of its permanent structure.

## Pulling It Together

A family is not like a rock that is permanently formed and fairly unscathed by outside influences. Our families are in a constant state of change. Members grow and mature. Life experiences change the individual members. So, we work to accept certain facts: people change, people experience difficulties, and we can only control our child to a certain degree. This results in a solid reality base that enables us to move forward creatively.

Accepting the fact that as parents we are human, make mistakes, and can only do the best we can adds a sturdy foundation to that base. Even if we were perfect parents, it is no guarantee that our children will have trouble-free lives (if we even wanted that for them). Remember, they aren't perfect either and will make mistakes from which they can learn. Accepting these terms gives us the best possible chance of becoming effective parents as we deal with the reality of parenthood and family life.

Also remember that as your children mature, each will have a unique perspective of what the family life was like. As you discuss family life and share viewpoints about the past, you may be shocked to hear that your children have interpreted a situation much differently than you or another child. One family I worked with had a father who grew up in an impoverished family. He had to work for everything he received. He could still feel the shame of going to school without proper clothes, and how he hated it when his parents argued over money. As an adult, it became extremely important to be successful. He made a great deal of money. He was determined that his children would have everything they needed. Money flowed freely between him and his children. He visualized this as a loving thing to do. His son, who was in treatment at the time for chemical dependency, believed that his father was "buying him off." That perception was as real to him as the motive of love was for his father. Only when they accepted each other's viewpoint did they start to heal the chasm in their relationship.

## The Journey's End

Our responsibility as parents is like creating a tapestry. The materials are there and we let the tapestry develop as we go along.

Each interaction between the members of the family adds to the design.

Your family is creating a tapestry, unique to its members. As the years go by, each individual adds to the overall failures and successes that are recorded on this tapestry. Each tapestry holds the family's history and imprint of each member. Not all families are alike—no two tapestries are alike. That makes each tapestry priceless. Take good care of it.

## References
Peck, M. Scott. 1978. *The Road Less Traveled*. New York. Simon and Schuster.

# About The Author

Carol Koffinke has been in counseling for fifteen years. The last five have been exclusively with chemically dependent individuals and their families. In addition, Carol has worked with the mentally retarded and their families, with adolescents in group homes, and as a guidance counselor for the U.S. Army. She has also been the director of the family program at Father Martin's Ashley, Inc. in Havre de Grace, Maryland.

Carol is a contributing author of *Treating the Chemically Dependent and Their Families* (Sage Publications, Inc.). She has also been commissioned by the Institute of Alcohol and Drug Studies for the State of Maryland to develop a course on "Relationships and Recovery." In 1975, she received her Masters Degree in Counseling and Human Services from Boston University.

Carol has lectured and conducted many workshops on family recovery and Adult Children Issues. She has appeared on public television and radio talk shows throughout the State of Maryland. Currently, Carol is the Director of Clinical Services for New Beginnings at Hidden Brook, an inpatient drug and alcohol rehabilitation center in Bel Air, Maryland.

# Other books published
# by
# DEACONESS PRESS

### Behind The Mask of Adolescent Satanism
*by Joyce Mercer*
*ISBN 0-925190-22-5, $9.95*

### When The Drug War Hits Home
Healing the Family Torn Apart by Teenage Drug Abuse
*by Laura Stamper*
*ISBN 0-925190-24-1, $8.95*

### What's Wrong With Me?
Breaking the Chain of Adolescent Codependency
*by Lonny Owen*
*ISBN 0-925190-14-4, $8.95*

### Designer Kids
Consumerism and Competition: When Is It All Too Much?
*by David Walsh, Ph.D.*
*ISBN 0-925190-12-8, $10.95*

### Little By Little, The Pieces Add Up
Daily readings for teens
*by Stephen Glick*
*ISBN 0-925190-11-X, $7.95*

### Relationships At Risk
*Assessing Your Kid's Drug Abuse Potential*
*by Timothy Titus, M.P.H.*
*ISBN 0-925190-02-0, $6.95*